Rothwell of Oldham

Sewing and Knitting Machines; Cycles; Motor Cars and Commercial Vehicles

John Warburton

John Warburton

F. Julia Dawson

Eclipse Publishing

Rothwell of Oldham

First published May 2010

Copyright © John Warburton 2010

ISBN 978-0-9565618-0-0

Number ......164.... in a limited edition of 600 copies.

Published by Eclipse Publishing, 1 Meadow Fold, Uppermill, Oldham, Lancs. OL3 6EZ

Printed and bound by Quorum Print Services Ltd, Units 3 & 4, Lansdown Industrial Estate, Gloucester Road, Cheltenham, Glos. GL51 8PL
www.quorumprint.co.uk

Dedication

To the memory of James Hartley Schofield (1909 – 1997), grandson of Fred Rothwell, who preserved and collected information concerning the Rothwell brothers' companies, and who in 1978 was the author of the first booklet on Rothwell history.

Contents

Foreword

My father was always proud to relate that he was a grandson of Fred Rothwell. Because of his long-standing interest in the early days of motoring in general, and especially in the motor cars and other machines manufactured by the Oldham businesses with which his forebears were concerned, Messrs. Shepherd, Rothwell & Hough and subsequently The Eclipse Machine Co. Ltd., he would have been delighted to know that they are now celebrated in this new book. But without his foresight in recording and preserving what few family records and photographs remained, the task of its writing would have been well nigh impossible. Using these records, my father wrote a booklet, *The Rothwell Car*, which was published in 1978 by the Oldham Libraries, Art Galleries and Museums as a Local Interest Centre publication, the first title to appear in the series, 'Oldham Studies'. It is now long out of print, but we acknowledge a great debt to this booklet. In truth, the book now in your hands is no more than a natural extension of that earlier work, but one that includes both material he was unable to accommodate through the restrictions present upon small scale publications thirty years ago, and an appreciable amount of relevant material that subsequently has come to light.

At the age of 22 in 1931, my father lost his job when his textile industry employers had to close down their business. Any kind of employment opportunity was rare at the height of the Depression, so he and another grandson of Fred Rothwell, his cousin Wilfred Rothwell Heywood, often known as Jerry, took out a lease on a small workshop in Oldham and set themselves up as garage owners and taxi proprietors. Each had received a legacy of £100 following the death in 1925 of their maternal grandmother, Fred's wife, Frances Rothwell, and the cousins used this as their capital. Servicing and simple repairs they carried out themselves, and they hired a part time mechanic for bigger jobs.

From this very modest start, the rest of my father's long career was spent in the motor trade, and with some success. In addition, he had a lifelong interest in motor sport and in the cars themselves. Through my father's business and the enthusiasm that he shared with many of his friends, I was brought up with cars and motoring, and classic and vintage cars have remained a constant presence throughout my life. Of course, it could be significant that my first name is Frances – I was so called after my aforementioned great-grandmother. In his old age, my father passed to me a couple of sales brochures for Rothwell cars and some albums he had assembled, containing early photographs of family Rothwell cars, all this amongst a good deal of other motoring memorabilia that he had collected over the years.

My special interest in the Rothwell cars remained dormant until an earlier contact with motoring writer, Michael Worthington-Williams was renewed in 1999. Mike researches and produces articles on the more obscure makes of motor car for specialist magazines, and he had already some years previously been in touch with my father with a view to writing a piece on Rothwells. In those days, there was no simple way of having old and precious photographs copied, and my father was reluctant to allow these treasured relics out of his possession. After my father's death, a chance contact through Bill Bishop, a friend in Australia who also happens to be a keen old car enthusiast, led to Mike and I getting in touch, and arrangements were then made to have good copies of my photographs produced. Mike asked John Warburton, a long-standing friend of his and another dedicated early vehicle enthusiast, to assist, and from our meetings was to come the collaboration that has resulted in this book.

Mike's article on Rothwell cars, entitled 'Oldham's Own', appeared in the monthly old car enthusiasts' magazine, *The Automobile* in December 2000, and it now seems that from that moment onwards, chance and enquiry have combined to create the most amazing treasure hunt. Firstly, down in Suffolk, Audrey Rothwell, the widow of one of my father's cousins with whom we had long lost touch, was told by her butcher that this article had appeared in the current issue of his old car magazine. Her imagination fired, at once she bought five copies, one for each of her four children and one for herself. She then contacted my family and the outcome has been a number of the happiest of social contacts.

In 1962, my father had bought the remains of what still is the only Rothwell car known to exist, as recounted later in this book, and local publicity led to a visit from William Boddy, the editor of the renowned national car enthusiast magazine, *Motor Sport*. His account of the car and the history of Rothwells appeared as an instalment in their series entitled 'Fragments on Forgotten Makes', back in their June 1963 issue. A reader in Kent then wrote to the magazine to say that his mother had an early Rothwell-made sewing machine, and enclosed a photograph. The editor had forwarded this letter to my father, who enquired if the machine could be purchased, but a reply revealed that the reader's mother still used it. There matters rested until, some 38 years later, John Warburton recognised the name of the *Motor Sport* reader on the letterhead, and, as a result, I was able to trace and then speak to him by telephone. I learned that his mother had died, but his father was still living with them at 96, 'deaf as a post', and the old sewing machine rested yet on their hall table. After a family discussion, the sewing machine came back to Oldham in return for a donation to a charity of their choice. Not only that, but it now stands in my home alongside a medal given to me by my father that had been awarded by the Oldham Agricultural Society back in 1879 to Messrs Shepherd, Rothwell & Hough for a 'collection of sewing machines'. What could be more appropriate?

This anecdote is recounted in some detail as an example of the remarkable coincidences, contacts and kindnesses that have led to me now having many more period photographs of

Rothwell cars, data on sewing and knitting machines made by Shepherd, Rothwell & Hough, the only known Rothwell bicycle, a gents' path racer made around 1902 and some original cycle sales receipts, and a marvellous 'Eclipse' treadle sewing machine in first class condition. I have also gained a much more extensive knowledge of my family's history. Each one of these discoveries has been a truly fascinating experience.

Another treasure hunt had the happiest of endings. Fred Rothwell's widow, Frances, had two pairs of stained glass windows made in his memory for St Andrew's Church in Middleton Road, Oldham where the family worshipped, and where Fred had served as a Trustee and as Vicar's Warden. They were installed in the south transept and dedicated in 1924. The church was demolished in 1982 as the district was cleared for redevelopment. More detective work and kind assistance led to these windows being traced to Hardmans', a stained glass works in Birmingham. After many upheavals and reversals I was able to retrieve two of the original four panels and have them replaced in conveniently blank windows in my own church, St Thomas's in Delph – which they fitted to perfection.

The greatest thrill of all has been the opportunity to acquire in November 2008 the 1910 20hp Rothwell car once owned by my father. The big adventure of 2010 will be to return it to the road after its lengthy slumber and mark its centenary by driving it down to the south coast and back, along a route taken in 1904 by pioneer motorists in a Rothwell car. This tour, and the full story of the last surviving Rothwell car are recounted in detail in the pages ahead.

The production of this book has been yet another fulfilling experience for me, satisfying my wish to see all this family material gathered together between two covers so that it conveniently can be shared with all those who have the same fascination as I have with a remarkable period in local history, and for the benefit and interest of future generations. I'm aware that it's a privilege to be able to draw attention upon the industry and enterprise that were so characteristic of the men and women of this small area of the north-west of England a century and more ago.

Finally, I owe a debt of gratitude to John Warburton, who edited the *Bulletin of the Vintage Sports-Car Club* from 2001 to 2008, for enthusiastically undertaking the tasks of research for, and the writing of this publication, and thereby enabling 'Daddy's book' to be enlarged and brought up to date. The Rothwell story can now be told in far fuller detail, and I hope – and, in fact, believe – that you will find it to be a most interesting account. My father would have been thrilled!

F Julia Dawson

Author's Introduction

A ride in a 1914 Humberette cyclecar at the age of 14 sealed permanently my schoolboy interest in veteran and vintage cars. Already, I had read most of the books on early cars that the local library could offer, made models of old cars, drawn them, and dreamed of the day that I might own even the most modest car from the 1920s or earlier. Thenceforth, matters concerning motoring history and the cars themselves have remained a constant part of my life. Inevitably, the 'O' word, 'O' for Obsession, has cropped up from time to time. But I am happy, I do not care, as I have been able to enjoy the satisfaction of restoring, researching and driving old cars, I've owned some outstanding examples and met many truly interesting people as a result of my passion. Many, too, are the valued friendships that have resulted.

Up to 1960, the books then available on vintage and veteran cars recounted the stories of the grand marques. The unique monthly enthusiasts' magazine, *Motor Sport*, was one of very few sources from which anything could be learnt about the more obscure makes of motorcar that exercised a particular attraction for me. 1960 witnessed the publication of Lord Montagu's book, *Lost Causes of Motoring*, and his Lordship's collaborator, Michael Sedgwick's research and scholarship most wonderfully filled this vacuum. The histories of all-but forgotten makes of car, such as Rhode and Squire, Crossley and Star, proved to be every bit as interesting as those of the famous makes of car.

I was aged 22 when I drove to Oldham in my 1920 Star tourer back in 1963 to inspect the chassis of the 1910 Rothwell car that had been reported in the local newspaper. Hartley Schofield made me welcome, and I was fascinated by his unique vehicle. Some years later, I saw it at an old car event, now restored with a reproduction touring body and looking quite magnificent. In 2001, I was editing *The Bulletin of the Vintage Sports-Car Club*, and, as editors ever are, I was eager to source good original material. A chance contact with Hartley Schofield's daughter, Julie Dawson, led to the motoring content of his home-published autobiography making a particularly pleasing article for the magazine, enhanced by some of the many period photographs that the family had carefully preserved.

Julie's interest in the various machines that her forebears had made long before her time led to further contacts, something of a meeting of minds, and a shared wish to see her material suitably presented for our own satisfaction, as well as – hopefully – the interest and enjoyment of others.

Acknowledgements

It is a fact that this book would never have appeared without the agency of my good friends, Mike Worthington-Williams and Tom Clarke, each of whom played a part in events that led to my introduction to Julie Dawson. They know the extent of my gratitude. My long-standing friends, Malcolm Jeal and David Hales, most willingly have contributed from their remarkable knowledge of early motoring history. Jean Sanders has helped greatly with genealogy, and Geoff and Norma Dickens with information on sewing machines. Martin Green has shared his expertise on early knitting machines, and Michael Green (no relation, I am sure) has been helpful with his detailed knowledge of his former employers, Messrs. Williamsons of Ashton-under-Lyne and their bell punches. Gordon Blaikie has tirelessly drawn upon his fund of knowledge of cycling history. Andrew Minney promptly provided excellent copies of company records of the Eclipse Machine Company and other concerns that are held by the National Archives, formerly the Public Record Office.

Many other friends and contacts have very readily given assistance, and it is true to say that no request that has been made has received anything other than the fullest response. Julie Dawson wishes to join me in our appreciation of Jane Gundry and the staff of Quorum Print Services Ltd of Cheltenham, who have taken special interest and care in the production and printing of the book.

Heartfelt thanks are also due to Geoff Ashton; Sean Baggaley (Curator, Gallery Oldham); David Baldock; Nick Baldwin; Nick Clayton; Tim Cork; Gowan Coulthard; Malcolm and Maureen Dungworth; Peter Fox (Curator, Saddleworth Museum); Frank Gilbert; Bryan Goodman; Tony Heywood; Jim McAndrew; Michael Megson; Ray Miller; the late Ron Sant; Rory Sinclair; Peter Stott; David Venables, and Jim Wood. Staff members at the Oldham Local Studies Centre, the Portland Basin Museum at Ashton-under-Lyne and at the Archives Department of the Museum of Science and Industry in Manchester, and Julian Jefferson and his staff at Touchstones, Rochdale all have gone out of their way to respond positively to our various requests, and their assistance is truly appreciated.

1. Introduction – the Rothwell Family

Oldham today presents a very different picture from that of a century ago: more so, indeed, than most other comparable English towns. From the 1850s until after the Great War, local businesses prospered in a manner unprecedented to that time and rarely seen since. It is sad that today, through changed circumstances, many of the fine buildings that reflected the municipal pride of those heady days have been demolished, or are closed and disused, and in some cases, in a state of shameful neglect. Inevitably, times change; the old employers with vast payrolls have gone, and have only in part been replaced in Oldham by smaller firms engaged in light industry and service businesses.

The prosperity of those distant years resulted in Oldham's rapid development, and many of the proprietors of leading manufacturing companies assumed positions of considerable influence in the town. Their families and colleagues supported the erection of the fine civic buildings, encouraged and were active in the arts and allied cultural and religious pursuits, and for the most part, could choose to treat their workforces in a paternalistic manner. Some of these local businesses such as Asa Lees and Platt Brothers, and from a later period, Ferranti and A V Roe achieved world-wide recognition.

Textiles were Oldham's foremost industry and many were the local businesses that were built upon the satellite needs of the giant cotton spinning and weaving mills and, centred in the Saddleworth valleys a few miles to the north, woollen mills. The figure recorded in the Oldham borough in 1913 for the workforce engaged in the mills was 35,000, with a further 28,000 hands in the adjacent districts. In fact, the proportion of the workforce that was *not* engaged directly or indirectly in the textile industry must have been quite small. 1919-21 saw a brief but wild boom in textiles, after which progress in the 1920s was erratic, with some spells of severe recession and part-time working. The major slump at the end of that decade brought widespread closures of businesses, unemployment, and financial ruin to some unfortunate investors. The few companies that survived those difficult years then struggled until the Second World War brought lifeline contracts for cloths, fabrics, woollen goods and surgical dressings. The damage occasioned by the Depression eventually was to prove terminal for many companies engaged in the textile industry. Accelerated by increasing quantities of cheap imports, the postwar years saw further rapid contraction of the textile firms remaining active across the UK, and especially in the many towns so engaged in the Lancashire and Yorkshire areas.

Maybe distance does lend a degree of enchantment, but the wide interest that so many people have today in local and family history, industrial archaeology and in the machines and products of days gone by, is more than mere nostalgia. In the absence of so many of the factors that we now take for granted, such as the internet, good lighting and clean air, better health care and safer working conditions and hygiene, the businessmen and workers of those days made,

Tom Rothwell at the age of 58 in 1904. (Gallery Oldham)

Fred Rothwell, circa 1900. The brothers were very alike in appearance.

through their industry and drive, products that embodied good traditional engineering practice. They employed skilled coach-builders, leather workers, sheet metal craftsmen and many workers experienced in other long-established trades and crafts. Their philosophy was: 'we have put the best of materials and engineering practice into this product; look after it and it will faithfully serve you for the foreseeable future.' Today, with planned obsolescence a familiar creed, we look back with some regrets to the days when coach painters applied by hand and rubbed down many, many coats of under-coat, top coat and finally brush-varnished the motor car bodies they had so carefully built....

The story of the Rothwell car gives a fascinating glimpse of the work ethic and

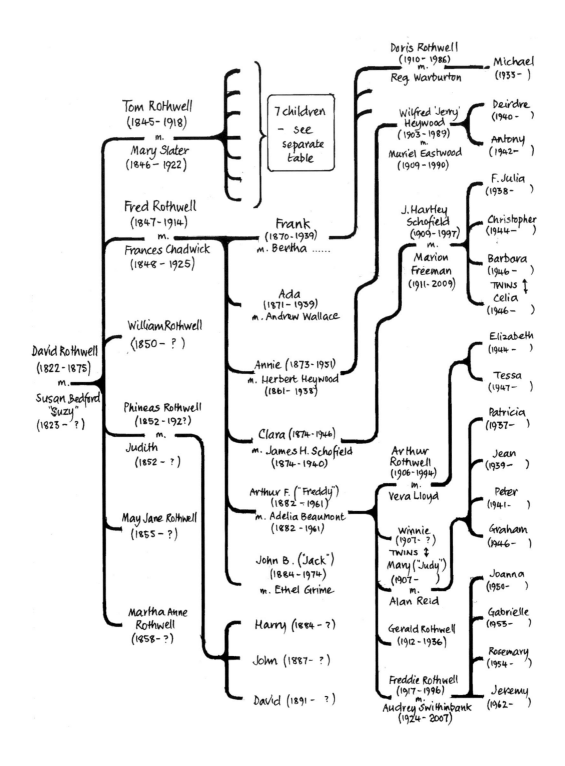

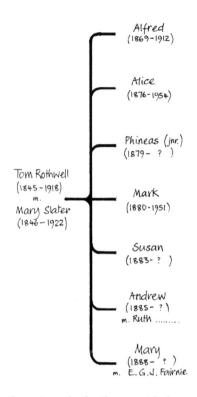

Alfred
(1869-1912)

Alice
(1876-1954)

Phineas (jnr.)
(1879- ?)

Tom Rothwell
(1845-1918)
m.
Mary Slater
(1846-1922)

Mark
(1880-1951)

Susan
(1883- ?)

Andrew
(1885- ?)
m. Ruth ....

Mary
(1888- ?)
m. E.G.J. Fairnie

Opposite – the family tree with three generations of Fred Rothwell's descendants. Above – sadly, it has not proved possible to trace Tom's descendants beyond one generation. Alfred, Alice, Andrew and Mark are known to have died without issue.

enterprise of our Victorian ancestors, qualities that enabled two mechanics of humble origin to become, in a comparatively short space of time, the owners of a thriving manufacturing business. Frederick (henceforth 'Fred') (1847 – 1914), the 19-year old younger son of David Rothwell, became an indentured apprentice to George Francis Bradbury and Thomas Chadwick, machinists of Wellington Street, Oldham on 12 December 1866, at a wage of sixteen shillings (80p) a week. The Wellington name was to be perpetuated by this firm, whose products went on to include sewing machines and then bicycles and motorcycles. As Bradbury & Co, their address continued as Wellington Works into the 1920s, the Iron Duke's profile portrait appearing on letterheads, and as transfers on their sewing machines, cycles and motorcycles.

'Bradburys' achieved no small fame, becoming one of the better-known makers of these machines in their day. Bradbury motorcycles were marketed between 1902 and 1924, and always maintained a reputation for quality and good finish.

Fred Rothwell's deed of apprenticeship with Bradbury and Chadwick ran for one year, indicating that he must already have served some years with another firm; no company would be likely to indenture a beginner as old as the age of nineteen. Fred's older brother, Tom (1845 – 1918), was apprenticed to Asa Lees & Co. Ltd., the famous Oldham firm of engineers and millwrights, as a turner. Their father's occupation is recorded as a 'mechanic – iron' in 1861. The census records show that by 1871, Fred had already married Frances Chadwick, but no relationship has been established between Frances's father John Chadwick and Fred's new employer, Thomas Chadwick.

In 1872, a partnership was formed between the two Rothwell brothers and two other local machinists, Emanuel Shepherd and James E Hough. They traded as Shepherd, Rothwell & Hough, initially from Matley's Buildings on the corner of Gas Street (now renamed Rhodes Bank) and Roscoe Street, off Union Street in Mumps, a district close to the centre of Oldham, where they manufactured sewing machines. Messrs Hirst, Kidd & Rennie, printers and publishers of the *Oldham Chronicle*, the leading local newspaper, occupied the Matley's buildings premises from 1930, and in a new building the firm remains on this same site to this day.

An outline of the Rothwell family's expansion can be culled from the ten-yearly census returns. David Rothwell, in 1851 a mechanic who had been born in Norland, Halifax in 1822, was living in Middleton Road, Chadderton with his wife Susan and their three sons Thomas (Tom), Frederick (Fred) and William, whose ages were 6, 3 and 1 year. Phineas was born in 1852. Ten years thence found the family living at Greenacres Road, Waterhead, Oldham, the occupations of young Tom and Fred (aged 16 and 14 respectively) both now being shown as 'mechanic – iron', as was that of David. By 1871, Tom and Fred were married and heads of their homes. Tom, an 'iron turner' and his wife Mary (née Slater), now lived at 3 Miles Street, St James's, Oldham, where their son Alfred was 2 years old. That same year saw Fred, a 'tool fitter' and Frances (née Chadwick) lodging at 118 Glodwick Road, Mumps, Oldham, this being the home of John and Mary Anne Chadwick, Frances' parents. Another 'boarder' was Emilina Temple, the Chadwicks' granddaughter aged 3. Frances' sister had married James R Temple in 1866.

Both Rothwell families expanded, and by 1881 Tom and Mary were living at 23 Orme Street, off Park Road, Oldham, their children now being Alfred, Alice, Phineas Jnr and Mark, aged between 1 and 12 years old. Tom's occupation was detailed as 'sewing machine manufacturer, employing 56 hands.' Phineas Jnr was the nephew of Tom and Fred's younger brother of the same name.

Following Tom Rothwell's family through, 1891 saw them living at 55 Belgrave Road, Oldham, and further children, Susan, Andrew and Mary had arrived. Some of the substantial houses of Belgrave Road still stand as reminders of a once upmarket residential neighbourhood, but the Rothwells' former home is one of many that have now been replaced with modern housing. Number 55 was demolished in 1990 and replaced by a detached house, a vicarage for the local parish. Ten years later, Sarah Slater, Mary's unmarried sister who had been living with the family in 1891, still was part of the household, but Mary, his wife, is absent. The most recent available census, that of 1911, reveals her as an inmate of the 'Prestwich Lunatic Asylum.' Mary Rothwell was to die there in 1922. In this 1911 census, Tom is a 'retired cycle and motor manufacturer' residing at Stoneswood, in Delph, and Alfred, Mark and Andrew are still living at home and engaged in the 'motor industry', Alfred being listed as an 'employer'. Alfred, unmarried, was to collapse and die, aged only 44, on 5 December 1912, whilst playing billiards at the Union Club.

Returning to 1881 and Fred and Frances' family, there were now four children, the eldest 10 and the youngest 7, and home was 64 Nuggett Street, Mumps. Ten years later, they had all moved to 39 Middleton Road, Hartford, Oldham, and Fred's mother-in-law, Mary Chadwick was now a widow and living with them. Number 39, along with all the other houses that once lined that side of the upper part of Middleton Road, is gone, and the area now an 'open space', grassed and planted with maturing trees and shrubs. Arthur Frederick (Freddy) and John Bedford (Jack) Rothwell had been born during the previous ten years, and were now aged 9 and 6. Ada (19) and Annie (18) were employed as 'fancy machine knitters', Frank (20) as a clerk and Clara (17) as a milliner's assistant. Fred is listed as a manufacturer of sewing and knitting machines.

When this Rothwell family group was taken in the early 1920s, Tom and Fred had died, and the Eclipse Machine Company was no more. In a summery snapshot so typical of that era, Fred's widow, Frances stands to the right, and between her son, Jack Rothwell and his wife Ethel is Ada Wallace, eldest daughter of Fred and Frances Rothwell. The car is Frances' 1915 15hp Rothwell landaulette.

The 1901 census sees Fred and Frances down in Bournemouth, staying at a hotel at West Cliff. A likely explanation is revealed by Clara's listing as a patient at the Sanatorium at Broomy, near Ringwood, where she was receiving 'out of doors treatment for consumption.' Aged 27 at that time, and 'living on her own means', it is pleasing to record that she did recover from tuberculosis, so frequently a killer in those days. In due course, she married James Hartley Schofield, and their son Hartley, Julie Dawson's father, was born in 1909. Clara Schofield died aged 72 in 1946.

Fred and Frances had moved to a new family home, 'Wilton Place', 10 Edward Street, by 1901. Edward Street was some ten minutes' walk from the works in Viscount Street. The two older Rothwell daughters, Ada and Annie, now aged 28 and 27 respectively, may well have helped at home – no occupations are listed. Freddy and Jack (John B), who now were 19 and 16, are employed as 'clerks at a cycle works' – doubtless, the Eclipse Machine Company. A further decade takes us to 1911, when only Fred and Frances remained at the family home. Fred is still recorded as an 'employer' and 'motor car maker', and Ellen Edwards from Holyhead was their 20-year-old servant.

2. Sewing and Knitting Machines, and Independence

From its outset 1872, the newly-established company of Shepherd, Rothwell & Hough offered a wide range of sewing machines, together with a surprising choice of case styles. Domestic models were proud possessions, and one of the larger treadle combinations was seen by its fortunate owner as an important and impressive part of the home furniture.

Two machines based on the successful Singer principle were made, the 'Family', priced at £6/10/-, and the 'Medium' at £1 more, both sizes being catalogued as the 'S' types. The 'Family' was in production from 1873 until 1889, and the 'Medium' appeared some ten years later. The Howe pattern closely mirrored the original design of that company, which was located at Bridgeport, Connecticut, and later also in Scotland. Howe machines featured their patent step or wheel feed, and were offered from 1873 to 1876 by Shepherd, Rothwell & Hough in three versions, A, B and C, which were priced between £7 and £8. Development was ongoing, as witnessed by patents obtained by the partners, two being registered in 1875. The first related to stitch length regulation, the second for an improved shuttle with adjustable tension. Worrall's Directory for 1875 carries their advertisement for sewing machines, and quotes their slogan 'All Others Eclipsed'.

Julie Dawson shows her table model Eclipse hand-operated sewing machine, and the medal awarded to Messrs. Shepherd, Rothwell & Hough in 1879.

Shepherd, Rothwell & Hough's trade mark was applied to their sewing machines, either as a colourful transfer as above, or as a stamping on the clothplate.

Three years later, a further patent was applied for; the specification described improvements in the control of both the underthread and the needle thread. A feature of the treadle machines made at this time was the perforated cast iron treadle plate that featured the capital letters 'SRH' centrally placed against a decorative background. Other, possibly later, machines featured the 'Eclipse' name in that same location. A new hand machine, of the Jones 'serpentine' form, was now introduced to their range. Shepherd, Rothwell & Hough also advertised heavy-duty sewing machines for shoe manufacturing; these were principally intended for the stitching of soles and uppers.

Perhaps indicative of their prowess in what was already a highly competitive field, the seven year old firm of Shepherd, Rothwell & Hough was awarded a medal at the Oldham Agricultural Society for a collection of sewing machines in 1879.

With a workforce now numbering 60 hands, the need became apparent for a more spacious factory. In May 1881, Shepherd, Rothwell & Hough's business moved from Matley's Buildings in Mumps to Viscount Street, about a mile away, just off the bottom end of Rochdale Road. These were newly-built premises and they were much larger, and the partners decided that a more impressive name for their factory, the Oldham Sewing Machine Works, better reflected the growth of their enterprise. As evidence of the firm's significant stature after some ten years in business, a surviving programme shows that on Wednesday, 4 January 1882, a Soirée and Ball was held in the factory premises themselves to celebrate the opening

The Eclipse hand machine by Shepherd, Rothwell & Hough, their Model 'S' in the Singer serpentine form, is the type of machine from which the firm's initial prosperity came.

of the Viscount Street works. The programme records that the Soirée was opened by Councillor Wild, JP, after which supper was served at 8.00 pm. This was followed by an Overture, a Grand March and seven set dances, interspersed with songs (one by Mr T Rothwell), recitations and a piccolo solo by a Mr. Schofield. There followed an interval during which dessert was served. The 'Part Second' of the evening's entertainment followed a similar pattern with a variety of vocal and instrumental acts, and must have continued well into the small hours. Those were the days!

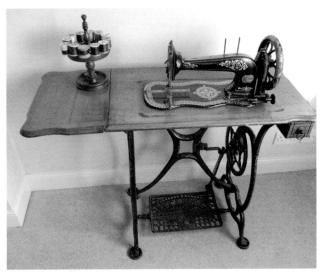

The fine 'Eclipse' treadle machine belonging to Julie Dawson. The treadle plate features the 'Eclipse' name and the machine predates the dissolution of the original company in 1887.

1885 saw the Eclipse Reversible sewing machine introduced. A final patent, obtained by Shepherd, Rothwell & Hough in 1887, was for improvements in driving and stopping gear for the crank wheels of both sewing and knitting machines. The partnership between the Rothwell brothers, Shepherd and Hough was dissolved in 1887 for unrecorded reasons. Tom and Fred Rothwell continued the business at the Viscount Street premises, initially

The medal awarded to Messrs Shepherd, Rothwell & Hough in 1879 by Oldham Agricultural Society for their collection of sewing machines.

SHEPHERD, ROTHWELL & HOUGH'S
"ECLIPSE" SEWING MACHINES,
OLDHAM SEWING MACHINE WORKS.

EVERY MACHINE GUARANTEED.

Machines for Families, Dress and Mantle Makers, Clothiers.

TRADE

MARK

Machines for Boot & Shoe Manufacturers, and General Light and Heavy Purposes.

"ECLIPSE"
A, B & C Machines.

"Eclipse" S. Machines.
FAMILY & MEDIUM.

ALL THE USUAL EXTRAS GIVEN.

STEP AND WHEEL FEED.

A. Machine	-	£7 0s.
B. „	-	£7 10s.
C. „	-	£8 10s.

FAMILY	-	£6 10s.
MEDIUM	-	£7 10s.

Cabinet Work in great Variety.

PROSPECTUSES ON APPLICATION OR POST FREE.

AGENTS WANTED IN UNREPRESENTED TOWNS.

The outstanding decoration an high quality finish apparent on an Eclipse treadle machine.

manufacturing the same products under the style of the 'Eclipse Machine Company.' James Hough moved south, where his interest in sound recording led him to join the Edison Bell Company in London; eventually he rose to become Managing Director. He died in 1925 at the age of 77. Emanuel Shepherd set up a sewing machine retailing and repair business on his own account, with premises at 41 Barker Street, Oldham, but this traded for only a few years because Shepherd died in 1894, aged only 48.

Domestic circular knitting machines, which were used principally for knitting woollen socks and scarves, had also been manufactured by Shepherd, Rothwell & Hough, and after the dissolution of the partnership, by the Eclipse Machine Company under the direction of the two Rothwell brothers. As well as providing for the needs of the owners' families, these machines offered the chance of generating some income, as garments could be knitted for sale to others. These small machines were clamped to the edge of a suitable working surface, such as a table, and were hand-cranked to operate them, and amongst the articles that also could be made were shirts, drawers, jackets, muffs, antimacassars, gaiters, babies' boots and much more. 'The most perfect Knitting Machine for Manufacturing or Domestic Use'. Fred Rothwell's daughter, Annie, became the demonstrator for this line, and also instructed purchasers on behalf of the company. A lively and emancipated red-head, Annie was also one of the first women in Oldham to ride a bicycle, an activity generally considered unladylike at that time. A 'rib-dial and circular knitter' made by Shepherd, Rothwell & Hough was a gold medal winner at the London International Inventions Exhibition held in 1885. A leaflet lists some 21 advantages claimed over other designs. Purchasers' endorsements of these knitting machines included one from the Prescot Union Workhouse, which

Stand 1,638, East Quadrant, Inventions Exhibition, South Kensington.

PATENT "ECLIPSE REVERSIBLE"

SEWING MACHINE.

The only Machine that will sew when turned in either direction.

The quickest and easiest Machine in the Market for Domestic and Manufacturing purposes.

It has fewer parts than any other Machine, and is consequently not so liable to derangement.

PRICE - - £7 10 0

These Machines are capable of being run at a higher rate of speed than any other in the Market; and are more durable, and less liable to derangement, in consequence of their extreme simplicity.

MANUFACTURERS:

Shepherd, Rothwell, & Hough,

OLDHAM SEWING MACHINE WORKS, OLDHAM.

The 'Eclipse Reversible' of 1885 was Messrs Shepherd, Rothwell & Hough's final flowering. (British Library)

Messrs Shepherd, Rothwell & Hough's 'Eclipse' knitting machine of 1885. (Museum of Science and Industry in Manchester)

gives an insight into other circumstances where such activities then took place. On 18 March 1886, the Workhouse Master wrote: " Sirs – Your Knitting Machine is giving us every satisfaction. We are saving money by every pair of hose and stockings made by it, besides finding employment for some of the infirm inmates. Two poor girls (cripples) and an imbecile have thoroughly mastered its use…."

In conjunction with Williamsons, the well-known ticket printers of Ashton-under-Lyne, the Eclipse Machine Co is believed to have manufactured some of the bell-punches then in universal use by tram conductors. With his son, Frank, Alfred Williamson (1837 – 1918) had designed and patented the Williamson bell punch, which they then supplied, along with other sundries such as leather cash collecting pouches, ticket clips and so forth, equipment that purchasers of their tickets would also need. Michael Green has researched the Williamson company, and his opinion is that the firm was principally a printing concern, and such sundry goods as they offered in their catalogues were sourced from outside suppliers. Michael has never found any link between Williamsons and the Eclipse Machine Company, but has evidence of other firms making

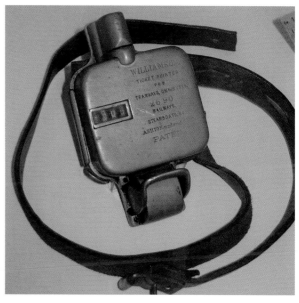

The Williamson ticket bell punch displayed at the Portland Basin Museum, Ashton under Lyne, Tameside.

metal goods for Williamsons. A similar but as yet undiscovered arrangement may well have existed with Eclipse, and claims of such were made long ago by Rothwell family members who were in a position to have had first hand knowledge.

The ticket punches certainly were stamped with Williamsons' name, and were listed at 4 gns (£4.20) each, or could be hired at a yearly charge of 15 shillings (£0.75). A Williamsons catalogue dated 1930 illustrates their ticket punches states that these had been offered by the firm for 'over 20 years.' It is reasonable to conclude that this arrangement was indeed a case of Williamsons subcontracting the manufacture of specialized engineering components to Eclipse under similar arrangements to those that they are known to have had with other suppliers.

Some reports state that the firm also made parts for the Edison Phonograph Co, and it seems reasonable to conclude that Eclipse was both equipped and ready to undertake the manufacture of smaller metal components for all kinds of domestic and portable machines.

3. Cycles and Motor Cycles

The middle of the final decade of the 19th century witnessed the peak of cycling's popularity. The far easier to ride 'safety cycle' with equal-sized wheels and a configuration still familiar today swept away the apprehensions of many would-be riders. Once members of the Royal Family were known to have taken up the pastime, society quickly followed. Sales to those sufficiently affluent to be able to purchase one of the new types took off, and existing manufacturers strove to deliver from overflowing order books whilst hopeful new makers sprung up in many towns. At this time the cost of a new bicycle represented a fair number of weeks' wages for the average working man, and ownership for many ordinary people had to remain a dream.

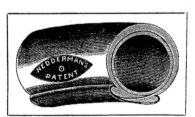

ROTHWELL CYCLES,

FITTED WITH

NEDDERMAN TYRES.

An early and apparently brakeless Rothwell gents' safety bicycle, perhaps a racing machine, from an Eclipse Machine Company advertisement, dated November 1892. Also shown are the overlapping beads and clincher rim of the Nedderman patent tyre, as fitted by Eclipse at that period.

The Eclipse Machine Company had been well-placed to join this throng, and had launched a range of types and sizes from about 1890. Their decision for this innovation could well have been prompted by recognition of a slowing down of the demand for sewing machines and an awareness that the recently introduced 'safety' pattern of bicycle was far more suitable for the hilly surroundings of Oldham than was the 'ordinary' type, commonly 'penny farthing.' No fewer than a dozen Eclipse cycles, all 'safeties', were displayed at the Stanley Show in November 1891, and the magazine, *Cycling*, commented that all were finished in the normal manner, with no extra touches for show purposes. The magazine also reported that Eclipse 'were hitherto known as makers of sewing machines, and had set up a new branch for cycle manufacture.' A surviving receipt dated June 1893 lists three machines delivered from the factory to the Grimsby depot, and quotes frame numbers 3060,

Miss M. HARWOOD.

"Winner of the recent Ladies' Six Days' International Race at the Aquarium on her "Rothwell." –
a magazine cutting dated November 1895: a sporting lady from the pre-Lycra days!

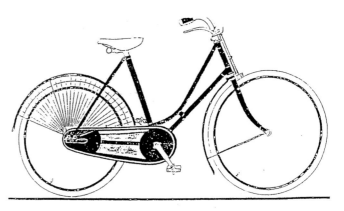

Rothwell Riders **ARE** free from trouble.

From a Rothwell advertisement of 1896 – a ladies' model.

W E Turner on his Rothwell track cycle circa 1885.

3079 and 3128, the latter being a 'semi racer' invoiced at £21. 'Cheques and P O Orders payable to T & F Rothwell.' The partnership promoted itself extensively, taking full page advertisements in the cycling press and had a stand either at the Stanley Show or the National Show in London until 1900. In their advertisements, the firm's boast was, "Rothwell Riders are Free from Trouble."

At the 1892 Stanley Show, the Rothwell brothers were reported as having at least six different types of cycle on display, including a ladies' safety with new pattern frame, and for traditionalists, a front driven 'safety' with Crypto gearing. All their diamond frame bicycles featured low placement of the bottom bracket in the interest of optimal stability. They had taken the patent rights to the Nedderman tyre, a beaded-edge type with

Right – R R Eglin (1872 – 1946) photographed in the 1890s, was a successful racer. First an employee of the Eclipse Machine Co., he later became proprietor of a cycle shop, and was a founding partner of Oldham Motor Co in 1907.

His great-grandson Robin M Eglin today is a director of OMC, upholding a remarkable family connection.

26

From 'The Wheeler' of December 1896, this general view of the Crystal Palace was taken during setting up of the various stands for the National Show, with the Rothwell stand visible, and evidently in process of being set up, on the left-hand aisle.

The completed stand is shown on page 28. (Both courtesy of Gordon W Blaikie)

The Rothwell stand at the National Show, Crystal Palace, December 1896.

Below – a receipt countersigned by R R Eglin for Dr White's Rothwell special gent's roadster, December 1905.

overlapping beads. The patent relating to this particular design was challenged by Bartlett, who held a patent on a similar type of tyre, and Nedderman lost. This must have had an effect on the Rothwells' company, but Dunlop soon became dominant in this field through buying all the important patents relating to pneumatic tyre manufacture, including the Bartlett one. By 1900, every cycle manufacturer fitted rims suitable for Dunlop tyres, these being of a type with which we remain familiar today. The firm continued to

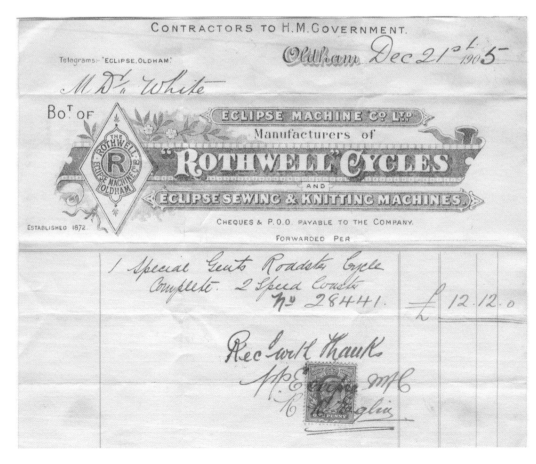

expand, a retail outlet was opened in Oldham and agents were appointed throughout the country.

The range of Rothwell cycles on Eclipse's stand at the Liverpool Show of June 1895 included a path racer and a road racer; a tandem and a ladies' safety, and the comment was 'high class machines in every way.' It has to be admitted that it was rare indeed for any exhibitor to suffer criticism in the periodicals of those days! Both potential and actual advertisers received a charitable press.

A large stand at the December 1895 Stanley Show featured twelve Rothwell machines, the most striking being a yellow-enamelled triplet. On a ladies' Rothwell, the rear hub had out-turned flanges to allow straight spokes to the hub. The National Show, held at Crystal Palace, London in December 1896, was fully reported by *Cycling*, and the Eclipse Machine Co. is referred to as 'a celebrated north of England firm.' The journalist continues to enthuse over their exhibits, whilst being unable to resist adding that Rothwells 'have eclipsed themselves.' All types were shown; gents, ladies and juveniles; tandems, triplets and tricycles. Detail improvements are described, and the writer gallantly says of the ladies'

The only known Rothwell bicycle – a gents' path racer of circa 1902. This machine is fully described in Chapter 8.

Below: close-up photographs of the well-preserved transfers on the above Rothwell bicycle.

models, 'every care has been taken that the rider shall obtain the most graceful position whilst riding commensurate with comfort.' Rothwells continued to be exhibited, and a late appearance was on the stand of Alexander & Co, of Niddry Street, Edinburgh at the February 1900 show in that city.

A larger depot had been opened in Grimsby by 1893 for the marketing of Rothwell bicycles in the eastern counties, and Fred's second son, Arthur Frederick (1882 – 1961), and always known as Fred or Freddy, was summarily despatched there in 1906 to manage it. Wild oats sown by Freddy had germinated…. His hasty marriage to Adelia Beaumont proved a very happy one, and she was a much-loved family member and a true 'character.' Hartley Schofield wrote of her, 'Not only was she a first class dressmaker, but also a marvellous hostess. She gave memorable parties, and was reputed to smash the dirty crockery rather than wash up after a successful evening.' Freddy served in the Royal Flying Corps during the Great War, and he and his family only returned from Grimsby to live in Oldham in 1922. Most confusingly, Freddy and Adelia's youngest son (they had five children) also was named Freddie (1917- 1996). Freddie – spelt thus – was to distinguish himself as a bomber and fighter pilot in World War II, after which a successful career in the RAF, commercial aviation and business followed, as detailed in Chapter 7.

After nine years of independent business following the dissolution of Shepherd, Rothwell & Hough, the Eclipse Machine Company became incorporated in October 1896, with nominal capital of £35,000 divided into £10 shares. With 1747 and 1748 shares each respectively, Tom and Fred held them all apart from single shares each to family members Alfred, Phineas, Frank and Ada, and likewise to the Company Secretary, Robert Cocks. Apart from a small holding of just 30 shares belonging to Cocks, family members still retained all the shares at the firm's winding-up in 1923.

The Eclipse Machine Co Ltd continued to make Rothwell pedal bicycles and tricycles into the early 1900s, but by then the cycle trade was in recession, partly due to the importation of cheaper cycles from the United States, and also in part due to disruption caused by the Boer War, as well as home market over-production. Rothwells no longer now took a stand at the major exhibitions so we may conclude that by the first decade of the 20th century, the firm was putting most of its effort into car production. It was the opinion of the late Ron Sant, an expert on cycling history and especially knowledgeable about those makes emanating from the Manchester area, that in all probability Rothwells continued to make bicycles until the firm closed. A Rothwell gents' path racer made about 1902 is the only bicycle of this make known still to exist.

In Hartley Schofield's autobiography, when he is discussing his days at the Grammar School in 1918, he writes: 'By this time, I had inherited the family bicycle on which I went to school each day. This machine, a Rothwell, of course, had a non-standard frame, and it was passed down from Wilfred to Arthur Rothwell then to me, and in due course to cousin Gerald and then on to Freddie! Its outstanding feature was the most excellent back-pedal brake, really powerful and trouble-free. I never understood why such brakes failed to become popular.'

Fred's son, Freddy, then aged 18, made an appearance in Oldham Borough Court in November 1899, the charge being that he 'unlawfully did furiously ride a motor tricycle'. The *Oldham Chronicle* reported the case, and Sergeant McGrath stated that the defendant at 9.20 on Wednesday night had driven a motor tricycle up Manchester Street 'at a terrific speed – at least 14 miles per hour.' The regulation maximum speed was 8mph, but the evidence presented stated that Freddy was travelling so fast that the Sergeant neither had time to speak, nor even raise his hand. Tom Rothwell, Freddy's uncle, spoke in his defence, suggesting that the noise the machine made could well have created an impression of greater speed, and he went on to say that, "If the trade was to be put down in this way, then they might as well sit down in Oldham and have no improvements." The exchange continued:

The Chairman: "That is another thing."

Mr Rothwell: "If motor cycling is going to be stopped in this manner, then it is going to become awkward."

The Chairman: "There are not many of them."

Mr Rothwell: "We are showing what can be done in the way of pulling them up and turning them quickly, in less time than with an ordinary vehicle."

The Chairman: "We are not trying the merits of the machine."

Mr Rothwell: "It is only capable at the very best road of going 12mph. It would not go up Austerlands at all."

The Chairman: "You have not made it quite perfect yet?"

Mr Rothwell: "We are having difficulty in getting up Manchester Street with it."

Amusing as this exchange may be, it is clear that motor tricycle manufacture was now being explored with serious intent by the Rothwells, and that Freddy was their chief test rider. This brush with the law cost Freddy 10 shillings and the Chairman observed that the Bench must protect pedestrians from those who drove too rapidly. 15 September 1904 saw Freddy at Bolton Petty Sessions, this time for failing to carry lamps on a 'light locomotive' on Chorley New Road, resulting in another fine. Only four days later, he was injured in an accident in Oldham, when his car skidded on setts that had just been watered, and collided with an electric tram standard, and 'he was thrown.' This particular vehicle was in fact BU35, a brand new 12 hp Rothwell dog cart, just purchased by local newsagents, Pollards, and it was 'considerably damaged.' Freddy was unconscious for some hours, suffered a broken leg in two places and was severely cut about the head. 'The horse ambulance was sent for.' He never did recover his senses of taste or smell. He was much more fortunate in December 1905, when the Commissioner of the Metropolitan Police exercised his discretion not to pursue Freddy for driving a motor car at a greater speed than 10mph in Hyde Park, but in September of 1906, he was summonsed to appear before Lytham County Court for driving a motor car at '31 miles 60 yards per hour' in Clifton Drive South, the speed limit being 20mph at that time. Again, he was lucky and escaped with a caution on that occasion.

At the National Cycle Show, Crystal Palace, 23-30 November 1900, Eclipse displayed their 2¾hp motor tricycle, and a few of these were sold. Rothwell motorcycles were also produced for sale, but in small quantities and apparently between 1901 and 1905. Little

ROTHWELL
The 2 h.p. ROTHWELL MOTOR CYCLE

"ROTHWELL"

DESCRIPTION.—This motor cycle is made with specially strong frame and forks, of graceful design, and is fitted with 2 h.p. motor, having mechanically operated valves, spray carburetter with throttle, ample space for petrol and lubricating oil, V shape belt, two brakes, etc., all combining to make it a thoroughly reliable and serviceable machine.

TERMS.

Cash with Order ...	...	£ 11 - 0 - 0
and Balance when ready for Delivery		£ 31 - 15 - 0
— or —		
Cash with Order	...	£ 11 - 5 - 0
and Balance in Twelve Monthly Payments of ...		£ 2 - 16 - 3

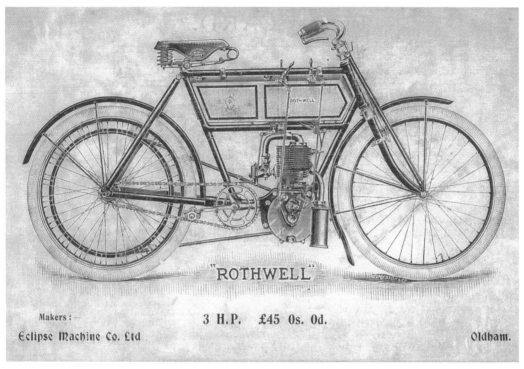

Makers :—

3 H.P.   £45 0s. 0d.

Eclipse Machine Co. Ltd   Oldham.

The catalogue entry, opposite, for the 2hp Rothwell motorcycle and the advertising card above for the 3hp machine each date from 1902-3. The 2hp is fitted with the Minerva 'clip on' engine, and the 3hp (above) has a Fafnir engine built into the frame.

information has been found, but two types were available in 1902-3, each powered by a different make of proprietary engine of 2hp or 3hp. The 2hp machine had a Minerva engine of Belgian design with mechanical inlet and exhaust valves and was marketed at £42/15/0; this type of engine was introduced in 1902. Such was their success that Minerva set up a branch here in the UK for engine manufacture. The 3hp model had a Fafnir engine.

The 2hp Rothwell motorcycle's Minerva engine was clamped below the front downtube of a 'diamond' frame closely similar to those of gents' roadster pedal cycles, and the engine's axis was inclined at 30° forward of the vertical. A spray carburettor was fitted and braking was by a cycle type stirrup brake on the front wheel rim. Belt drive was provided, running direct from an engine crankshaft pulley to a belt rim incorporated in the rear wheel spoking, as was common practice at that period. Of course, this gave one speed only, and there was no provision for a clutch: if the machine stopped, the engine stopped too. Pedals and a cycle-type chainwheel and sprockets were used for starting, and also for the application what euphemistically was termed 'light pedal assistance' on uphill grades when the power unit began to falter. Most probably, only experimental machines were made initially, with some measure of series production becoming established by 1902. The overall design of these motorcycles was conventional for the period.

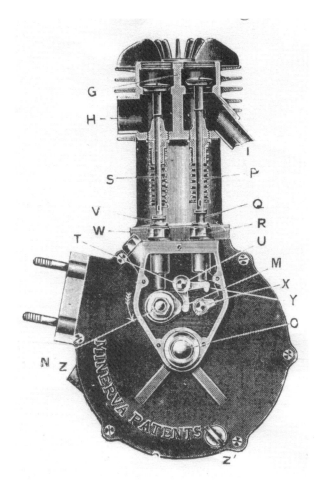

The Minerva 2hp engine of 1904-3 was advanced in that it featured an inlet valve opened by the camshaft: automatic inlet valves were more common practice at this period. The exhaust valve is opened by a rocker arm actuated by the camshaft lobe, and the inlet valve directly. The fixing clamp location is seen on the left of the crankcase.

The Fafnir proprietary engines fitted to the 3hp Rothwell motor-cycle were imported from a manufacturer of that name in Aachen, Germany. The increased power of this engine necessitated a more robust frame construction with the engine mounted vertically, its crankcase spanning the open lower part of the frame, which was braced with an additional crosstube below the fuel tank. The Fafnir engine design featured an automatic inlet valve whereby the suction of the descending piston pulled open the inlet valve against a weak spring, to admit the mixture from the carburettor, which in turn had drawn warm air from around the finned cylinder barrel. The front forks had reinforcing struts fitted. The 3hp Rothwell seems now to have been a better buy at £45, offering a worthwhile increase in power and in some respects a better specification for the modest extra premium of £2/10/0 (£2.50) over the cost of the 2hp.

A surviving early machine that is claimed to have been sold under the Rothwell name has features predating either of the two foregoing patterns, of which catalogue illustrations exist. This machine has a 1¼hp Minerva engine of 211cc. with an automatic inlet valve, clamped to a frame little removed from that of a conventional bicycle, although the front forks do have reinforcing stays. Barring the rumoured existence of another early Rothwell motorcycle still in the hands of the family who purchased it new, this intriguing machine could be the only remaining tangible evidence of Rothwell's motorcycle venture.

The Eighth Annual Cycle and Motor Show in Manchester took place during the first week of February 1904, and The Eclipse Machine Co. displayed their Rothwell cycles and motorcycles, 'all of excellent design and finish, attention to detail being very marked', in the opinion of the *The Cycle and Motor Trader*. Either cars were excluded from this show despite its title, or this magazine restricted its review to the cycles and motorcycles displayed.

In comparison with their production of motor cars and commercial vehicles, the Rothwell brothers' involvement with motor cycle manufacture was a mere flirtation. The total number of Rothwell motorcycles made is very speculative. Some nine machines have been located in surviving registration records, none of which was issued later than mid-1905. With production apparently largely contained within three years, the total might have just have exceeded three figures. The engine horsepower, where stated in these records (see Appendix 1), in certain cases is inconsistent with known types. One machine is recorded (W135, January 1904 in Sheffield) with a 2¾hp Whitley proprietary engine. This Coventry firm was in business from 1902 to 1910, and, whilst predominantly

The 3hp Fafnir engine did feature an automatic inlet valve, seen here with a relatively sophisticated carburettor connected via a short inlet tract.

making parts including engines for sale to other motorcycle 'manufacturers' ('assemblers' in reality), did themselves make and sell a number of complete machines.

Two makes of motorcycle were sold under the name 'Eclipse', and neither has any connection with the Eclipse Machine Company of Oldham, or, indeed with each other. An Eclipse motorcycle was produced by John Bright of Birmingham between 1903 and 1905, which had a novel and advanced feature, a variable speed gear. And in 1912, Job Day & Sons Ltd of Leeds produced motorcycles that they marketed as Eclipses. Designed by H A Smith, they had 499cc engines with overhead inlet valves. Job Day & Sons made packaging and slicing machines and also produced the Day-Leeds light car between 1912 and 1924.

Another potential cause of confusion when considering motorcycles and pedal cycles marketed under Eclipse or Rothwell trade names is the existence of two companies

Seen in 2007 in the late Roger Field's private museum, this machine shows a number of modifications but remains the only known motor cycle with a claim to the Rothwell name.

registered to Bolton addresses that were in all probability mutually linked. The Rothwell Machine Company of Market Street in Bolton – only some 20 miles west of Oldham – operated in a similar line of business, offering sewing and knitting machines, and was also listed as 'importers of cycles, tricycles, tricycle carriers, cycle accessories and various parts thereof.' This firm was in business from 1899 to 1904, when it was wound up by a court order, and their products are described and illustrated in contemporary cycling periodicals. They were agents for both Seyfert and Donner loom-type multiple knitting machines: these were large commercial installations. The Company Secretary of the Rothwell Machine Co Ltd was William Rothwell Jnr. A second firm, with an address just round the corner in Knowsley Street in Bolton and also first registered in 1899 was Fred Rothwell & Co Ltd, with F Rothwell as a managing director. The Rothwells concerned here in Bolton lived either in that town or in nearby Horwich, and no connection has been identified between them and the 'Oldham' Rothwell families or businesses.

4. Rothwell Cars – Getting Under Way

Fanny Chadwick, a sister of Mrs Frances Rothwell, the wife of Fred, had married James Temple, whose father for a time was employed as a coachman to George V, the last King of Hanover (1814-78). King George of Hanover was a male line descendent of the British King George III and a cousin of Queen Victoria: in fact, until Queen Victoria's first child was born in 1840, he was second in line to the British throne. Completely blind following an accident in 1833, he divided his time between England and Germany, but following political upheavals in 1866, he spent the rest of his life in exile in Austria. It would seem that Temple's employment created a link with Germany that would have a significant impact upon Freddy Rothwell's education.

Late in 1893, Fred Rothwell had sent Freddy, his second son, to be educated at the Neuenheim College in Heidelberg. His schoolmaster there, Mr Armitage, clearly was British and oversaw other English boys. A letter dated February 1894 written by Freddy to his family back in Oldham mentions solid-tyred German bicycles, and he asked for his cricket bat to be sent to him! This German connection was to have a far-reaching effect on the Eclipse Machine Company, for Fred, no doubt whilst on a visit to Heidelberg to see his son, was interested to inspect a Benz 'Velo', one of the first successful motor vehicles. Whilst sewing machine sales were steady, the cycle trade was very seasonal. The Rothwells were eager to keep their workforce fully employed during the slack period of the winter months, and this led them to investigate the possibilities of motor manufacturing. The brothers decided to obtain a car to examine, and, Fred, recalling the Benz, arranged to purchase a 'Velo', at the time these being best selling motor vehicle in the world. The records of the Daimler-Benz Museum in Stuttgart confirm that in April 1897, a 3½hp. Velo, 'Patent Motor Wagen No. 510' left Mannheim for their English agent, Arnold's Motor Carriage Co, 59 Mark Lane, London EC. The maker's brass identification plate from this very early car still exists in Julie Dawson's possession via her father, but nobody knows what became of the Benz.

The Benz 'Velo' was a true horseless carriage, a two-seater with solid tyres on large diameter wire spoked wheels, the rear ones much larger than the front wheels, and the engine, a water cooled open crank single cylinder of 110 x 110mm bore and stroke, was located at the rear of the vehicle with the cylinder lying horizontally. The flywheel was vertical and was pulled over by hand to start the engine. A small steering lever sat on top of a vertical steering column, and other levers mounted below

A 3½hp Benz 'Velo' of the type purchased in 1897 by the Rothwell brothers. (Malcolm Jeal)

shifted the belt to alternative pulleys to select either of two forward speeds, and final drive was by side chains. Unlike a number of other pioneer car makers, the Rothwells appear not to have made close copies of the Benz, but no doubt they used this early car to gain experience of the internal combustion engine and motor driving, and possibly also to learn what might be best avoided in motor car design.

In 1898-9, the Rothwell brothers had a typically unsatisfactory encounter with the American entrepreneur and acknowledged charlatan, Edward J Pennington. Along with The Protector Lamp & Lighting Co, a not-dissimilar smaller firm located in suburb of Eccles on the opposite side of Manchester from Oldham, The Eclipse Machine Co. was engaged to make parts for Pennington's light motor vehicle, the 'Victoria.' The Protector Lamp & Lighting Co's principal activity was the manufacture of Davy-pattern miners' safety lamps, but in the early days of the 19th century, they did market some motor cars under the trade name of 'Bijou'.

A small and faded snapshot showing Freddy Rothwell at the wheel of the first Rothwell car, in Edward Street, Oldham.

Pennington's very small four-wheeled vehicle was colloquially known as the 'Raft', and weighed only 2¼ cwt. It featured front wheel drive via rope transmission, 'a twelve foot rope joined by a long splice', and was tiller-steered to the rear wheels (the rear track was appreciably narrower than that of the front wheels), and was advertised at a bargain price – below £100. The engine was claimed to develop 3½hp and was centrally placed below the floorboards and was described as having a single horizontal cylinder of 3¼in bore and 8in stroke, with a horizontal flywheel of 32in diameter. The frame itself was without any suspension, the seat being sprung above it. One was exhibited at Crystal Palace in November 1898, but no mention was made of the part that the two Lancashire engineering companies had played in its construction.

Sam Lomax and John Norris in their book, *Early Days*, on the beginnings of the motor industry in the Manchester area (privately published in 1948), were very charitable indeed when they stated that the Pennington 'Raft' Victoria was 'too far ahead of its time to be a practical proposition with the manufacturing facilities then

THE ROTHWELL LIGHT CAR.

THE accompanying illustration shows a new light car which is about to be put on the market by the Eclipse Machine Company, Ltd., of Oldham. Power is supplied by a 6 h.p. vertical petrol engine, which is placed under the bonnet in front, and is supported on a strong underframe, as are also the gear box and countershaft. The cylinder is water-cooled, the circulation being maintained by a pump. The gears provide three forward speeds of seven, fourteen, and twenty-one miles per hour, and one reverse motion; from the countershaft to the rear live axle the power is transmitted by a strong chain. Two powerful and independent band brakes are fitted, either of which

is sufficient to hold the car on any hill, and we understand that they act equally well in both directions. The body is hung on springs independent of the motor and other mechanism, so that there is practically no vibration when the car is stationary and the engine running. The illustration shows a two-seated body, but we understand that future vehicles will have accommodation for four persons. Inclined wheel steering is fitted, and all the changes of speed are controlled by one handle working in a notched quadrant. The road wheels are all 26in. diameter and fitted with pneumatic tires. The weight of the car complete is 7¾ cwts.

From the Motor Car Journal *of 9 November 1901 – the first press announcement of a Rothwell car.*

available.' In the event, no more than three of these vehicles were completed by Pennington & Baines, the latter being Pennington's British agent, but hundreds of orders had been taken, and Pennington beat a hasty retreat to the US in the October of 1899, very possibly accompanied by the deposits taken. The Rothwells were left holding a considerable quantity of now useless parts intended for the unorthodox 'Raft', but the company survived the setback of this abortive venture.

The Motor Car Journal of 9 November 1901 announced the first four-wheeled motor vehicle to be sold under the Rothwell name, a light car which had a 6hp front-mounted vertical water-cooled single cylinder engine, almost certainly a De Dion Bouton unit, in a tubular frame. Water circulation was pump assisted, a gearbox provided three forward speeds and reverse, and the live rear axle was driven by a single roller chain from a countershaft. A subframe carried both the engine and gearbox, and two separate brakes

A puzzle – this car appears to be a twin-cylinder Darracq of 1903, but no such are recorded in the Oldham 'BU' records. Fred and Frances pose in the Lake District with their grandson, 'Jerry' Heywood, who was born in 1903.

were fitted. The body in turn was supported on coil springs and the 26in wire wheels were fitted with pneumatic tyres. For that year, an inclined steering column topped with a steering wheel was an advanced feature. An article published in 1912 commented that some of these first Rothwell cars must have still been running at that time, as the firm occasionally received orders for spare parts for them.

The next development was the introduction of two new types, a different 6hp single cylinder model, and a 12hp twin-cylinder. The new 6hp cars were on the market by April 1903, and appear to have been assembled from proprietary parts. They featured De Dion Bouton engines of 90 x 110mm bore and stroke (700cc) fitted in chassis purchased from the well-known French suppliers, Messrs. Lacoste et Battmann. Described as a 'popularly priced vehicle', the Rothwells must have come to realise that a car assembled from

tried and tested proprietary components could be sold more cheaply and with greater confidence than one built by them to their own designs, and would return better profits. The 'De Dion – Lacoste & Battmann' formula was commonly adopted by many of those joining the ranks of 'motor manufacturers' at that time. The 6hp Rothwell weighed 8½cwt and had a short

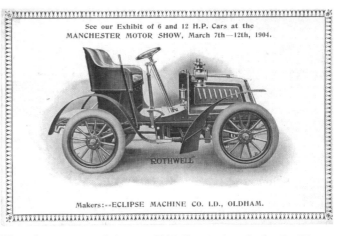

See our Exhibit of 6 and 12 H.P. Cars at the
MANCHESTER MOTOR SHOW, March 7th—12th, 1904.

'ROTHWELL'

Makers:--ECLIPSE MACHINE CO. LD., OLDHAM.

This advertising card shows a 1903 6hp single-cylinder De Dion engined Rothwell with quadrant gear change lever mounted at the side. Frames and axles came from Lacoste & Battmann.

wheelbase – 6ft 3in. By June 1904, the 'coal scuttle' pattern of bonnet fitted to the first 6hp Rothwells, with the gilled tube radiator suspended below the front frame cross-member, had been superseded by an angular bonnet with parallel top and side panels that fitted over a similar type of radiator but now mounted above the frame, giving an appearance not unlike that of contemporary Gladiator and Speedwell cars.

During 1904, the 6hp Rothwells gained a repositioned radiator ana a new design of bonnet. This example was registered to Ernest Robinson of Dobcross on 20 June, and was painted green. From 1913 it was in Ashbourne, with its fifth owner.

Below – nothing is known about this late 1904 10-12hp twin-cylinder Rothwell. This model shared some features with the contemporary Darracq cars. A fine photograph!

This 10-12hp Rothwell was the first of three cars of the make purchased before 1914 by J W Ray of Liverpool. He owned a business that manufactured ships' instruments and fittings such as engine room telegraphs. Here, his two sons pose with this rear-entrance tonneau-bodied car of early 1905. The younger boy's pedal car bears the same registration number!

The twin-cylinder cars bore a resemblance to the current successful Darracq models. Both 6hp and 12hp models appeared at the Manchester Motor Show in March 1904, the twin-cylinder car having an Aster type 24K proprietary engine (88 x 140mm bore and stroke), a French-made unit widely used at the time, and this type continued into 1905. *Peach's Annual* for 1905 lists two models of Rothwell car, a single cylinder now of 8-9hp and probably again with a De Dion engine, and a twin cylinder 10-12hp, which had

replaced the earlier 12hp. Expert motoring historian, Malcolm Jeal has identified the engine fitted to the new 10-12hp 'twin' as another type of French proprietary power unit, the 100 x 120mm Vautour. Messrs Montauban et Marchendier of St Quentin, Paris, made engines up to 100hp and also gearboxes, marketed under the trade name, 'Vautour' – French for 'vulture'. The 10/12 had a radiator shaped not unlike the early Rolls-Royce cars and placed a little forward of the front axle and clear of the bonnet. The 8-9hp Rothwell appears to have continued to be sold in small numbers for another couple of years. In 1905, it was priced at £235, and four prices are quoted for the 10-12hp; £255,

Right – the early 1905 10-12hp Rothwell chassis, and, below, its 100 x 120mm (1885cc) engine, a Vautour proprietary unit. (Malcolm Jeal)

£275, £300 and £325: presumably the first being the chassis price and the remaining three figures for coachwork of increasing complexity – the catalogue does not elucidate. London agents were appointed – the Balcombe Motor Co of 12 Marylebone St, NW. Organised by various bodies, motor shows were regular features, even in the early days of the 20th century. The first appearance of Rothwell cars so far discovered at one of these occasions was their stand at the fifth show of the Society of Motor Manufacturers and Traders (SMMT), this being held at Crystal Palace, London in November 1905.

This 10-12hp Rothwell was registered on 24 July 1905 to John Stuttard of Windsor Road, Oldham. It formed a Christmas card sent to their friends in December 1906, this example franked – and, doubtless, delivered – on 25 December!

A revealing aside to the Rothwell car story occurred in August 1904. Appearing in the *Oldham Chronicle* was an account of a 'wakes week tour' by 'four Oldham gentlemen including the owner of a Rothwell motor-car of 12hp.' 'Wakes

weeks' were the annual fortnight's holiday of industrial areas, when all the mills and even local shops and businesses closed down, the smoke-laden atmosphere present for the rest of the year cleared, and mill workers relaxed – and, if they were fortunate – departed by train for a few days at the seaside.

On this Rothwell car, the four pioneer motorists left Oldham at 6.10am on the Saturday morning and made excellent progress southwards, covering 136 miles during that day to finish at Worcester. En route, the motoring holidaymakers had passed through Sandbach, Crewe, and Whitchurch, then Shrewsbury and onwards via Much Wenlock and Kidderminster. Even today this would be a very daunting run in an early car. In the main, the following days were less strenuous, and after staying at Weymouth on the Dorset coast, they turned east. Excursions had been made to Stonehenge from Salisbury in the car, and then by ferry to the Isle of Wight from Portsmouth. Heading back north from Chichester, the return journey took them through Guildford to Windsor, then by way of High Wycombe and Blenheim Palace to Stratford on Avon. The final two days took the Rothwell's crew home to

Another view of members of the Ray family of Liverpool in their 1905 10-12hp Rothwell tonneau.

Oldham, but not by any direct route – first by Kenilworth, Coventry and Tamworth to Shrewsbury again, to stay the Saturday night in Ellesmere, and finally a shorter run home on the Sunday, arriving at 2.25pm. 'Little or no trouble with the car' was reported, although the water pump gland had needed repacking at an earlier stage, a trivial matter indeed, and 'no accident, never even ran over a chicken but very near running down a pig.' The full text of this 'pleasant and exhilarating run' is included in Appendix 3.

Family lore has it that this car belonged to one or other of the Rothwell brothers, but in the reserved manner of the day, no names are quoted in the newspaper article, nor was its author identified. By August 1904, only four 12hp Rothwell cars had been registered in Oldham, and one of these, BU15, to the Eclipse Machine Company, and that would seem to be the most likely candidate to have been the car used on this adventure.

BU37, a 12hp tonneau-bodied car was registered to Fred Rothwell on 1 November 1904, which he kept until 1906. The next owner of that car is recorded as Joseph Lafaille of Antwerp, whose travelling acrobatic troupe was then appearing at Oldham's Theatre Royal.

5. Four-Cylinder Rothwell Vehicles

A J Adams, a draftsman who previously had been in charge of the drawing office section of Royce Ltd in Cooke Street in Manchester, was employed from August 1905 as the Eclipse Machine Company's designer. He had been involved with the first Rolls-Royce cars, which had appeared in 1904. Rolls-Royce was to move to Derby in 1908. Adams' contribution in Oldham resulted in the introduction of a series of larger Rothwell cars from early in 1906, with either of two main sizes of engine, the 20hp, quoted originally as 20-24hp, and the 12-14hp. The single cylinder De Dion-engined Rothwells and the twin-cylinder Aster and Vautour-engined cars gradually were phased out over the next two or three years.

The Adams-designed 20hp engine was to be the mainstay for the rest of Rothwell car production. The cylinders were cast in two pairs and the inlet valves were enclosed in cast iron domes above each block; each cover was detachable by undoing a single nut. The larger castings were supplied by the local Oldham firm of Dronsfields at Atlas Works, who also purchased some Rothwell vehicles, including 20hp chassis with light commercial bodies. Side exhaust valves were fitted, all the valves being operated from a nearside camshaft, the inlets via external push-rods. The crankshaft was carried in five phosphor bronze main bearings. The engine had a bore and stroke of 4in x 5in (102 x 127mm, giving a swept

The 20hp Rothwell engine, designed by A J Adams.

*From the sales catalogue for 1907, this '25hp Rothwell with detach-
able brougham top' was one of the first examples of the new 'Adams'
model made, and probably shows BU58, supplied to John Murgatroyd
of 'Stoneswood' in Delph, and registered on 15 February 1906. The
staggered spoke Mulliner patent wooden artillery wheels were a
feature of the more expensive form of the Rothwell chassis.*

volume of 4,152cc) and, running at 1,000 rpm, developed 25 bhp. Much less sophisticated were the lubrication arrange- ments – even as late as 1910, the oil pump remained remote from the engine, driven by a leather belt from a pulley at the rear of the camshaft. This delivered oil from a smallish underbonnet tank to a gallery of drip feed sight lubricators, which metered lubricant that then passed down copper pipes to three locations on the engine, plus the gearbox input bearing. The engine lubrication operated on the total loss 'splash' system with big-end dippers into the oil in a close-fitting sump. It is possible that by 1912 the more expensive Model A 20hp cars had acquired an oil pump driven direct from the camshaft, possibly even down in the sump, but the catalogue description, whilst implying a change from the 'bootlace' driven pump, is unclear.

A skew-gear driven cross-shaft at the front of the engine drove the magneto (offside) and the distributor for the coil ignition (nearside). White & Poppe or Zenia carburettors were fitted (the latter on the more expensive chassis type), mounted on the offside, this location being changed to the nearside by 1910. Dual ignition by trembler coils and high tension magneto was provided, the two completely

*John Murgatroyd (at the wheel) purchased BU71, (registered on
15 May 1906), and sold both his home and this fine 20hp touring
car to Tom Rothwell later that year. The steps lead up to
'Stoneswood's entrance, and remain unchanged to this day.*

separate ignition systems servicing the two sparking plugs provided for each cylinder. The trembler coil ignition offered the benefit of easier starting, and once the engine was running, the coils were switched off and the engine normally ran on magneto only. The engine was supported in the frame from below by a pair of cradle cross-members, the engine mounting lugs being integral with the lower half of the crankcase.

Cooling was by thermo-siphon aided by a flywheel fan, the engine compartment being sealed by an undershield. The first radiators 'possessed novel features, inasmuch as they are formed from 200 lengths of coiled copper tube, each coil being about ten feet in length.' This design was patented, and was claimed to provide a cooling surface between two and three times greater than that of other patterns. The copper tubing was 0·1875in diameter with a wall thickness of 0·015in.

Power was transmitted through a leather-faced cone

Seen outside his home, 45 Queens Road, Oldham, overlooking Alexandra Park is a '12hp Aster-engined' Rothwell 'side entrance tourer, dark red, lined cream', registered 26 May 1906, and purchased second hand by George Ingham in August 1907. The engine was a twin-cylinder. (Michael Megson)

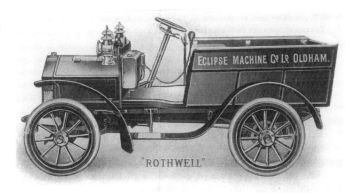

A 10-12hp 'light delivery car', with Aster engine; circa 1906. The steering column gearchange and solid rubber tyres are notable.

clutch to a separate gearbox, the gearlever, on the driver's right, being spring loaded towards the centre plane of the gate, which was notched to prevent jumping out of gear. A sub-frame carried the three speed gearbox. A live rear axle was fitted; the differential, which was enclosed in an aluminium casing, was of the spur type. Alternative axle ratios were offered to suit different districts or the type of coachwork to be fitted. The rear wheel brakes

Registered to the Eclipse Machine Company on 8 November 1907, this 'green 20-24hp' touring car with Mulliner wheels was retained as a demonstrator for some years. One of the two Rothwell brothers sits next to – presumably – a grandchild for this summery photograph.

A 1907 15hp White & Poppe-engined Rothwell used to transport the comedian George Robey between his music hall engagements.

were internal expanding, and the foot brake shoes also operated internally within a drum on the transmission behind the gearbox. The propeller shaft was open.

Suspension was by four semi-elliptic leaf springs, with a further transverse 'platform' spring at the rear for some models and at various times, and grease cups were fitted to some shackle joints, others being drilled for oil can lubrication. Worm and nut type steering was employed, the box not being sealed to contain the lubricant. Stripping was necessary to lubricate the steering gear, a feature shared with the 40/50hp Silver Ghost and the earlier 20hp Rolls-Royces – Adams' lingering influence, perhaps? The pressed steel frame was

George Ingham's second Rothwell, a 20hp tourer painted dark green, purchased new and registered on 8 April 1908. Again, the setting is Queens Road. (Michael Megson)

narrowed in front to give a conveniently small turning circle. Ground clearance, at 8½in, was more than adequate. The petrol tank was housed beneath the driver's seat, feeding by gravity to a White & Poppe carburettor. The chassis was sold with a six month parts warranty, and a comprehensive tool kit was supplied with each vehicle.

An interesting experimental development had been the firm's constant-mesh gearbox, which was very silent in operation. The gears were engaged by means of sliding keys, but unfortunately this design had to be abandoned because of the frequency with which the keys sheared.

The majority of the engine and chassis parts were made in the company's own works in Viscount Street, where the standard catalogued open two- or four-seater touring bodies were also constructed, trimmed and coachpainted. Either model was available as 'chassis only' for purchasers who wished to make their own arrangements for bodywork, as was common practice at the time. Specialist coachbuilders such as Joseph Cockshoot and William Arnold of Manchester made bodies for both models, usually the more elaborate types, such as landaulettes.

The firm was one of the early members of the Society of Motor Manufacturers and Traders, and Rothwells were to exhibit their cars at all the Olympia Shows in London, which were restricted to members of the SMMT, from November 1905 until 1912. Provincial shows were also held in Birmingham, Manchester and Scotland, and Rothwells usually appeared locally.

When a group of six local businessmen got together and set up the Oldham Motor Company in 1907, Fred Rothwell was one of them. The other founding directors of Oldham Motor Co were Ralph Rothwell Eglin, a cycle dealer, C G Bullough, a confectioner; F Smith, a cotton doubler; George Ingham, a rope manufacturer; and W T Cooper, a

Two of the 20hp vehicles supplied to Dronsfields, the local iron foundry and engineers who supplied larger castings to the Eclipse Machine Company. Both light lorries were registered in 1910, a delivery cart in crimson to the left, in July (BU252), and BU262, a 'cart body, grey, lettered gold' in October.

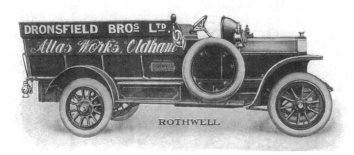

From an advertising card, and possibly showing the very vehicle on the left in the upper photograph.

butcher – in fact, nobody with a direct link to motor manufacture apart from Fred Rothwell. Initial agencies held by the OMC included Humber, Rover, Argyll – and Rothwell cars. This firm of motor dealers went from strength to strength in the following years and today is a very large and successful dealership offering all the expected services. The new Ford factory at Trafford Park, Manchester opened in 1911, and Oldham Motor Company were quick off the mark, being appointed Ford Agents on 6 October that year. Fred resigned from the OMC Board in 1910, his place being taken by Charles Hardman, who later was to become a mayor of Oldham, and who also owned a Rothwell car. The reason for Fred's resignation is long forgotten. Maybe he came to feel that there was a conflict of interest as his co-director Ralph R Eglin was an agent for Rothwell bicycles, among other makes. In the 1890s, Eglin, a noted racing cyclist, had been employed in the offices of the Eclipse Machine Company and ran the firm's main retail outlet for Rothwell cycles from premises at 72-74 Yorkshire Street. The Eglin

Buckley & Prockter was Oldham's leading department store. Above is a late 1905 12-14hp Aster-engined chassis, and below a 20hp, probably BU269 of 1910.

connection with OMC spans 103 years, as today Robin M Eglin is an OMC Director. Oldham Motor Company has been exclusively a Ford dealership since 1922.

Making sense of the different models offered through the years relies upon surviving sales catalogues and the all too infrequent listings of data in the weekly motoring magazines, particularly those issues describing the exhibits at the various motor shows. The task is not assisted by Rothwells, in common with some other car manufacturers, themselves being inconsistent when referring to what clearly was the same model, by using differing ways of expressing the horsepower ratings.

Following through first the smaller and then the larger series of four-cylinder Rothwell car models from 1905, we find that for 1906-9, the smaller car, designated the 12-14hp, had a 'T' head (the inlet and exhaust valves on opposites sides of the engine, operated by separate camshafts in the vault of the crankcase) of 80 x 90mm bore and stroke, and this was a proprietary engine made by Messrs. White & Poppe. Wheelbase options were 8ft 2in or 8ft 6in.

For 1908, a new smaller four-cylinder Rothwell called the 15hp made its brief appearance and had the 84 x 110mm Aster proprietary engine (*The Autocar* of 26 October 1907 quotes 88 x 140mm for the Aster-engined 15hp Rothwell). The 15hp in 1907 shared the track and wheelbase (9ft 3ins) of the 20hp, and neither the 15hp nor the 20hp had the extra transverse rear 'platform' spring of the concurrent '25hp' (that being a higher-specification chassis but fitted with the familiar 20hp engine). The 15hp, at a chassis price of £295 cost only £5 less than the 20hp. 1909 and 1910 saw the 15hp Aster-engined Rothwells dropped, but a new 15hp had appeared by April 1911, with 80 x 127mm dimensions, and this differed from the Adams-designed 20hp engine and featured side-by-side valves in 'L' head formation, and the crankcase was mounted in the frame by conventional side extensions. In the absence of any contradictory information, it is assumed that this engine was of Rothwells'

J W Ray's second Rothwell, a 20hp tourer, new in July 1909.

Although no catalogue description has been found for chain drive Rothwell commercial vehicle chassis, some were made. If the lorry above is BU171, it was a 20hp vehicle made early in 1909.

Seen at the Manchester Show in February 1912 is this chain drive Rothwell commercial chassis which offered a 35cwt carrying capacity against 20cwts of a similar chassis with a bevel rear axle. The heavy duty wheels carry Dook-Swain solid rubber tyres.

own design. Adams had departed by 1907, one report stating that his next employers were Messrs. Cockshoots in Great Ducie Street, Manchester.

An undated sales brochure for Rothwell commercial vehicles, but probably circa 1906, gives options of two sizes of Aster engine, namely 10-12hp or 12-14hp (£10 extra): of the details and dimensions of these engines, nothing more is revealed than, 'This well-known engine scarcely needs description, being so thoroughly known for its reliability and efficiency in working'. That's all! These light commercial chassis had a steering column gearchange below the wheel, and live axle drive, both types of design being well known as Darracq features. Illustrations of commercial-bodied Rothwells dating between 1907 and 1914 show clearly that the bodies were mounted on the normal 20hp touring car chassis, but one enigma exists – a photograph of a heavy ambulance for the St John Ambulance Brigade which is built on a much more substantial chassis with longer wheelbase, twin rear rims, and the radiator has cast aluminium sides and a header

One of the most handsome Rothwell cars. An example of the 15hp model reintroduced during 1911 with a completely different engine. This new and unregistered car is straight from the paint shop, and awaits fitting of its lighting set. The upholstery is protected with detachable canvas covers.

tank of the same material with 'Rothwell' script in relief; a far larger vehicle in every way. From the registration records, it is known to have had the usual 20hp engine. It must have been built late in 1914, but no reference relating to this type appears in any catalogue specifications or in articles in contemporary periodicals.

Adams' new '24hp' Rothwell had appeared for the first time at the aforementioned November 1905 SMMT show at Crystal Palace. In November 1906, Rothwells put on a more extensive display at Olympia, with three complete cars. On display were a double landaulette and also 'double side entrance' bodywork, each on a '20-24hp' chassis (the familiar 20hp again), the engine of which, plus the crankshaft, camshaft, axles and other parts were also separately displayed. The White & Poppe-engined 12-14hp with Roi des Belges open coachwork was stated now to have a pressed steel chassis frame; previously this model had featured an armoured wood chassis.

For 1908, and as displayed at Olympia in November of the previous year, the '25hp' continued, and a chassis and a complete car with a landaulette body, and a '20hp' with side entrance. At this time, the '20hp' and '25hp' names were given to models that shared the same engine, but in the case of the 20hp, it was fitted in the lighter chassis of the 15hp. The 15hp also was shown in chassis form with the 84 x 110mm Aster engine with separate cylinders, and dual ignition was fitted to all models. The 15hp had pump-assisted water circulation, thermosiphon sufficing for the larger model. The chassis price of the '25hp' was

£450 against £300 for the '20hp', and the more expensive cars had 12-gallon, as opposed to 6-gallon, fuel tanks. The '25hp' had a most unusual feature, namely wooden artillery wheels with two rows of spokes, 20 spokes in line in the felloes, but staggered into the hubs at the front, and 24 spokes in the rear wheels, similarly arranged. This pattern of road wheel was a Mulliner patent. The cheaper model had conventional wooden artillery wheels with half the number of spokes. All Rothwells had 3-speed gearboxes.

A tubular front axle was noted as a new feature in descriptions of their 1909 Show exhibits, destined to prove a short-lived innovation, and a 20hp chassis again was on display, this time with the gearbox lid removed. Another point to attract favourable comment was the crankcase windows provided to expose to view the connecting rods, big ends and crankshaft. The 25hp again is described as a different model. In November of 1910, the descriptions of the exhibits on the Rothwell stand reveals no change, but now a different agent in London is listed – W G James, of '4 Mortimer Street, W'. Two complete side-entrance cars and a 20hp chassis were displayed. A year later, once more no significant alterations are revealed, only 20hp cars were shown, one of them in bare chassis form. The transverse rear spring and White & Poppe carburettor receive comment.

At Olympia in November 1911, the new 15hp makes its bow, with 79 x 127mm bore and stroke, paired cylinders, pump lubrication to main bearings and troughs into which the big end caps dip. The new 15hp had a wheelbase measuring precisely 9ft. A 15hp chassis was shown and a two-seater with folding rear seat, finished in French grey and lined in green, and also a third 15hp Model B, with flush-sided torpedo touring body. Also shown was a '28hp' D-fronted landaulette – '28hp' being yet another description of the familiar Adams 20hp.

The 1913 models were on display at Olympia in November of 1912, and *The Autocar*'s journalist clearly was barely

Above – a 15hp two-seater, 1911, seen against a typical Oldham background.

Below – its completely new power unit.

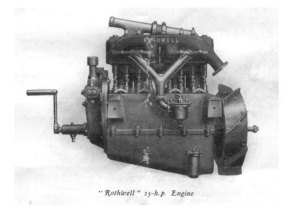

"Rothwell" 15-h.p. Engine

The car which makes friends
wherever it goes. . . . .

CHASSIS.

15 h.p.	20 h.p.
15'5 R.A.C. rating,	25'6 R.A.C. rating,
£285.	**£300.**

The "Rothwell" Car is made entirely at Oldham in Lancashire: — from whence all good things come. Around its home the roads are hilly and cobbly, and being brought up in a hard district, its reliability is absolutely number one, and its efficiency A 1; never mind the others.

MAKERS:
THE ECLIPSE MACHINE CO., LTD.,
OLDHAM.

The
"Free from Troub'e" Car

ROTHWELL

An advertisement of January 1912.

suppressing a yawn as he anticipated Rothwell's display: 'This is one of the cars that we seldom see or hear of except at Olympia. We are not advised of any improvements for the coming year, so that it will suffice to say until we have had the opportunity of examining the cars, that they are both four-cylinder models….. Both have 'four speeds' and both are claimed to be of the same weight of chassis, though how this may be, we do not profess to understand.' With the following week's issue came a slight decrease of world-weary boredom – the gearboxes were now correctly described as having three forward speeds, and reported to be displayed on the stand were a 15hp chassis and another 15hp with two-seater body, plus a pair of 20hp cars, one with a Kelvin four-seater body and the other with the standard flush-sided tourer body. November 1912 proved to be Rothwell's Olympia swansong, doubtless to the relief of *The Autocar*'s man.

Although only the 20hp was listed in 1910, confusion became confounded by the firm offering the 20hp in 'Model A' and 'B' options for that season. Again, the same engine was fitted to the both the 'A' and 'B', but the 'B' was cheaper by a factor of a chassis price of £300 to the £400 of the 'A', but the cheaper model perpetuated the chassis dimension differences of the earlier '20hp' cars. The 'B' could be had with a choice of three rear axle ratios, yet only two options were listed for the 'A' and the latter had a larger rear tyre size, yet –

J W Ray at the wheel of his third Rothwell car – a 20hp tourer of 1912. During the Great War, he fitted a large gas bag above the car and continued to run on town gas.

oddly – the catalogue shows the cheaper 'B' with Warland detachable rims: the 'A' had fixed wheels and therefore lacked this useful feature.

The Rothwell brothers must have held up their hands in acknowledgement of criticisms about the lack of clarity in their sales literature over the differing specifications of the Model 'A' and the Model 'B'. On the face of it, with each using the same engine, the justification for the very considerable difference in chassis price is far from clear. In an attempt to explain, a footnote appeared below the chassis specification of the 20hp Model 'A' chassis in the sales brochure issued for the 1912 season. It read, "Although in the general specification this model appears somewhat similar to our Model 'B' Chassis, yet it is an entirely different production and design. The frame is longer and wider, and upswept at the rear to give clearance for the rear axle. The springs are made longer and more flexible, both front and rear axles are of a heavier and more expensive type, the wheels are larger and fitted with 880 x 120 m/m tyres and the whole of the operating mechanism is different. Altogether it is a more expensive chassis and finished in the highest class, and is to be recommended when the fitting of a large, roomy, and comfortable body is desired."

Whilst nothing is revealed in the text of the 1910 sales brochure to differentiate, close inspection of the illustrations of the Models 'A' and 'B' does show many detail differences

This much heavier 20hp Rothwell commercial chassis was bodied by Bury firm, Wilson & Stockall, and registered DK589 and marked 'war service', on 14 January 1915. (Nick Baldwin)

BU721, Mrs Frances Rothwell's 1915 landaulette is immaculate through Harry Fletcher's care. Jack Rothwell stands behind, and the setting is Grasmere's Rothay Hotel in the summer of 1920.

between the frames, steering, axles and bracketry of the two types. The axles of the Model 'A' had a track some 5in wider than the 'B', and the more expensive chassis also featured a cast aluminium bulkhead, whilst timber sufficed for the Model 'B'.

In 1910, the open cars were supplied with folding Cape cart hoods at an extra charge of £10, and £18 for the two- or four-seater types. The normal finish of all bright parts was polished brass, but nickel plated finish could be supplied at an additional cost of £7/10/0. Lamps, speedometer and horn were also extras, and optional equipment also included a Stepney spare rim and tyre. Rudge-Whitworth wire wheels could be provided in place of the standard wooden artillery wheels. It is interesting to note that customers nervous of their car running backwards after a missed uphill gear change could have a drop-down sprag fitted for £1, an archaic feature in 1910. Another period touch is that the charge for crests and monograms was quoted at 10s 6d each.

Although no factory production records survive, it seems likely that up to 1914, about 500 cars had been produced, some of which were exported to South Africa, and one, finished in primrose yellow, to India for the use of a civil servant. Appendix 1 lists details of some 124 Rothwell cars known to have been registered in the UK, culled from

On the same Lake District holiday in 1920 – Mrs Frances Rothwell's 1915 15hp landaulette and family members – from the left, Mrs Annie Heywood; Frances (seated); Mrs Clara Schofield; Mrs Ethel Rothwell; James H Schofield; and Harry Fletcher, chauffeur, in his cap and dustcoat. The open touring car behind is Jack Rothwell's 30hp Daimler.

End of an era – Jack Rothwell's car was one of very few Rothwells built immediately after the end of the Great War, and was registered on 7 January 1919. Hartley Schofield attacks a sandwich with schoolboy gusto, whilst Clara, his mother, busies herself with their picnic.

various sources, and it is acknowledged that there must have been many more. Even this incomplete list of data is adequate to give a fair indication of a number of trends.

Of the Rothwell cars listed in Appendix 1, the 6hp singles and 12hp twins appear to have been produced up to 1906 in approximately similar numbers, with the larger proportion of the singles of the earlier days giving way to more 'twins' latterly. From 1906, the 'Adams era' cars, the larger with his engine and the smaller with White & Poppe or Aster engines,

BU894, Jack Rothwell's green 1918 20hp Rothwell touring car, in which he covered 19,000 miles.

start to come through, and 1907, 1908 and 1909 are shown as active years, with roughly equal numbers of the smaller and larger models being registered. From early in 1910, the 20hp is universal, as at this period, no smaller model was offered. Strangely, only one of the later type 15hp models appears in the listing before the beginning of 1915, DK251, a tourer registered in Rochdale in June 1911. Photographs exist of other 'late' 15hp cars, and the likely explanation is that most were registered in towns, cities and counties where the records are lost or not researched.

It is interesting to note that Rothwell cars were to account for over 25% of all vehicle registrations in the Oldham district between the years 1903 and 1910. The list shows that during the War years the few vehicles that left the factory were mainly lorries and vans. After the Armistice of November 1918, the last four private cars appear, three 20hp cars and a single 15hp, plus a 20hp

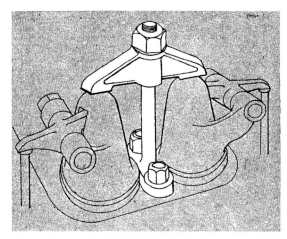

Adams' signature – the inlet valves of adjacent cylinders in their cages retained by a single nut and steel yoke arrangement. See photographs on page 80.

lorry, these vehicles in all probability having been assembled from existing stocks of parts.

By the time that Fred Rothwell died in July 1914, car production at Viscount Street already seems to have fallen off markedly, and both the Oldham and Rochdale vehicle records, which show the influx of Model 'T' Fords being registered by that time, must point to one good reason why this was so. Whilst the outbreak of war was a national crisis and many able bodied workers enlisted to serve in France, War Department contracts secured by the Eclipse Machine Company would appear to have saved the firm in the nick of time.

The expensive £400 Model 'A' Rothwell chassis as illustrated in what could have been the last sales brochure the Eclipse Machine Company produced, not dated, but probably issued for the 1911 season.

6. The Great War and Death; Contraction and Closure

Fred Rothwell died on 22 July 1914. His obituary notice stated that his death followed prolonged illness, and family memories are that the cause of his death was lead poisoning. Wilton Place, 10 Edward Street, Oldham proved to be the final family home for Fred and Frances. He had remained a director of various local businesses including the Heron Mill, the Iris Mill, the Bell Mill and the Times Spinning Co. On their marriages, he had bought fine new homes for each of his daughters. His children inherited shares in the business. His estate had a gross value of £49,841, net £49,784; this latter sum having a 2010 purchasing value of £2·15 millions – no Inheritance Tax in those days! Whilst that was a substantial fortune, the captains of Oldham's leading manufacturing firms of the late 1800s had left estates up to ten or twenty times greater.

In his memory, Frances, his widow, had two pairs of stained glass windows designed by Fred's son-in-law, James Herbert Heywood (known by his second forename) and made by the famous Manchester firm of glass craftsmen, Leylands. Herbert Heywood was a prominent local architect and his best-known commission was planning the layout and buildings of the Oldham Garden Suburb. The two pairs of windows showed Biblical scenes: firstly, Christ raising Lazarus from the dead, and secondly the scene at the Sea of Galilee where He told the fishermen that He would make them 'fishers of men.' The quality of these windows was – and remains – outstanding, with rich colours and a strong art nouveau influence. They were installed in St Andrew's Church, Middleton Road, Oldham, where the family worshipped and where Fred had been a trustee and former vicar's warden. The windows were dedicated in February 1921, and Julie Dawson was to save them in recent times, as recounted in Chapter 8.

For relaxation, one of Fred's favourite haunts had been the West End Bowling Club, situated on Selkirk Avenue, then in a prime residential area of Oldham. Crown green bowls, snooker, billiards and card games all were accompanied by a lively social scene, and the membership of the West End club included many of the influential personalities of the local business and professional community. Fred was elected President of the West End Bowling

Oldham's West End Bowling Club – seen in 2008 and still going strong .

Club in 1902, an honour also bestowed upon his son Frank in 1917. Fred's daughter, Clara, Mrs James H Schofield, was a great fund raiser for the club, and threw herself into organising many social events there. In recognition of her work, she was elected an Honorary Member in 1925 – the first lady to receive this distinction. At the time, the Schofields lived in some style at Hartford Cottage, in Grange Avenue, and James Schofield, too, was elected President of the Bowling Club, serving in 1922 and 1923. The Schofields were one of many families in the Oldham area fated to lose all their money in the crash of 1929-30; they left the district and lived out their days in a modest home on the Fylde. Hartford Cottage was demolished in 2008.

Of the two Rothwell brothers, Tom took by far the larger part in civic life, and served as a Justice of the Peace in Oldham from 1903. He had been elected a local Councillor back in 1895, serving for 3 years, followed by a further term from 1904. He was appointed an Alderman in May 1907 and sat until 1913. Tom was a director of a number of mills in the Oldham area, including the Times, Devon, Lily and Olive Mills. Latterly he too suffered poor health, and he died at Stoneswood, his home in Delph, at the age of 73 in January 1918. He remained Chairman of the Eclipse Machine Co to the end of his life. Tom left £31,479 gross, net £27,891, and the changed financial climate of the final year of the Great War saw the net figure's purchasing power today being around £642,000. Much of his shareholding had been passed to his children some years previously.

Looking back to those days, men who had a hard and long working life were truly 'old men' when in their sixties, and in the cases of both Tom and Fred, their drive and commitment to the firm must have been declining from 1910 onwards, possibly reflected in the apparent drop in motor vehicle production figures of 1913-14. The prolonged hospitalization of his wife, Mary must also have been an additional burden for Tom.

Chadderton Cemetery contains many testaments to the prosperity and social status of prominent citizens of Oldham's industrial past. Numerous vast and elaborate tombs and memorials line a walk to the left, close to the main entrance. Here are found those of Tom and Fred, adjacent to each other in death as they had been in life. Some of their descendants share their graves. Tom and Mary are inscribed on Alfred's magnificent marble headstone, highly elaborate and some 10 feet high, clear evidence of the couple's devastation at the sudden and premature death of their eldest son at the age of 44 in 1912. As the eldest

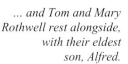

The memorial to Fred and Frances Rothwell in Chadderton Cemetery...

... and Tom and Mary Rothwell rest alongside, with their eldest son, Alfred.

Rothwell of his generation, Alfred would surely have been seen as the principal heir to the business. Fred and Frances's headstone is hardly less impressive.

On the outbreak of war, production at the Viscount Street factory was turned over to the manufacture of material for the armed forces, chiefly grenades, Mills bombs and shells, with only the very occasional motor vehicle or cycle being assembled from parts in stock. Very many thousands of steel darts were made, these to be showered over enemy lines from aircraft – a particularly gruesome form of attack and one reminiscent of the archers of Agincourt. The letterhead of the Eclipse Machine Company, typically ornate as was the fashion of the time, had included the wording, 'Contractors to H M Government' since at least 1902, suggesting that the wartime manufacturing contracts were an extension of existing and relatively long-standing arrangements with military authorities.

A Mr V Platt worked for the Eclipse Machine Company during the 1914-18 War; his father A V Platt having been manager at the firm before 1909. In a letter that he wrote to Hartley Schofield in 1966, the younger Mr Platt recalled a limited number of ambulances and wagons being made for the War Office. Very few indeed are the Rothwell vehicles that appear in the Oldham registration records during this period, additional evidence that vehicle production was an occasional and subsidiary activity in comparison with the firm's munitions contracts.

Prior to the outbreak of World War II, the few surviving Rothwell cars had vanished from the roads. There's no doubt that many Eclipse sewing machines were still stitching furiously in 1939, and likewise numerous Rothwell cycles were being pedalled along by proud owners, but, for almost every one of these, their days too were numbered…

7. Subsequent Family History

By 1914, the greatest proportion of new vehicles registered in Oldham were Fords from Manchester's Trafford Park factory, a development that cannot have been lost on the Rothwells. The 15hp Rothwell introduced in 1911 was barely more up to date in concept than the ageing 20hp, and the Rothwells must have become increasingly conscious of the need to introduce a completely new design if the firm was to continue in the motor manufacturing business.

It seems clear that the wartime contracts were profitable and gave the firm a new lease of life. In the autobiography he complied in 1982 for his family, Wilfred 'Jerry' Heywood wrote: 'The 1914 – 1918 War had been a gold mine for the Eclipse Machine Company. I remember going to the works to help prepare for the sale of machinery and stock: it seemed such a shame that the family business was being allowed to lapse in this way.' Fred and Tom had had the drive to oversee the sound establishment of their company, but their increasing age and health problems appear to have begun to have an impact on the business in the last two years of peace. Tom was 66 and was listed as retired at the time of the 1911 census, and Fred had died in harness in 1914. By the end of hostilities in 1918, Tom too had died. The next generation of Rothwells at the forefront were Fred's sons Frank (48), Freddy (36) and John Bedford Rothwell (always known as Jack, who was 34), and Tom's sons Phineas, (39), Mark (38) and Andrew (34). Hartley Schofield knew most of this generation of Rothwells, and recalled Freddy as being a particularly attractive character, but it seems that none of the men had either a compulsion or the talent to assume leadership.

There must have been many family discussions, along the lines of 'Where now?', but the evidence suggests that the sons, quite understandably, were daunted by the major commitment clearly necessary if cars were to continue to be made. At the same time, the appeal of the option of winding up the company and sharing the considerable assets would have been undeniable.

This path was adopted, and in 1923 the formalities were finally completed. It would appear that this was a paper exercise that followed some considerable time after the works were closed down, machinery and stock dispersed and maybe even the premises sold. Jack Rothwell's share of the proceeds was sufficient to keep him and his wife in some affluence for the rest of his long life – he never worked again, always ran two cars up to the Second

World War, and died in 1974 aged 90. His investments must have been far more fortuitous than those of certain other family members who lost almost all their invested money when severe recession in the spinning mills in the later 1920s was exacerbated by the impact of the 1929 stock market crash. Their wealth had been invested in textile stock, much of which collapsed to the extent of becoming valueless. In fact, some types of shares were only part paid on issue, the company concerned remaining in the position of being able to call in the balance at a time of their choice. When hard times did come, choice became necessity for struggling textile firms, and those shareholders holding part paid shares found themselves in liability and could have to pay others to accept their shares and then assume the liability for current and possible future calls.

Freddy Rothwell was described by his son, likewise Freddie, but spelt differently (1917 – 1996) as 'intelligent but impractical'. He went bankrupt in 1930, after which time he and his family were supported by his eldest son, Arthur (1906 – 1994), who had emigrated to America where he had then become successful in business.

'Young' Freddie went on to have a distinguished career in the RAF during WWII as a bomber and fighter pilot, being awarded the DFC in 1943, and thereafter served and then found high level employment in many countries, including India, Thailand and Kenya. Freddie served as Equerry to Princess Alexandra on her Asian Tour. He was also put in charge of the reception here in Britain of the many Ugandan Asians expelled from that country by General Idi Amin. He was appointed CBE in 1971.

In her husband's Will, Frances Rothwell inherited the last car Fred had owned. In December of 1915, she purchased a 15hp Rothwell landaulette BU721, which she then used for the best part of ten years, always immaculately presented and maintained by her chauffeur, Harry Fletcher. Harry had been excused war service as he had only one eye. He was forbidden by his employer ever to exceed 15mph on pain of dismissal but despite this, numerous family holiday photographs of the early 1920s show this car in locations in North Wales and the Lake District, doubtless reached after interminable journeys.

Frances Rothwell sold 10 Edward Street in 1921, moving to a smaller house on Grange Avenue, and some 18 months later, after an illness, she went to live with her daughter Clara Schofield. Not long before Frances' death in 1925, her 15hp Rothwell was exchanged for a 15·9hp Humber landaulette. To the end, she had maintained her habitual accompaniment to luncheon – a glass of claret and a glass of water.

8. Existing Rothwell Artefacts and Locations

Language ever evolves, and so the word 'Rothwelliana' can be welcomed as an ungainly newcomer! Julie Dawson has a collection of Rothwell and Eclipse bill heads and paper-work, and many photographs of Rothwell cars. Also included in the collection are John B Rothwell's 1904 driving licence, and a fine leather bound notebook in mint condition, with 'Rothwell Cycles' gold embossed in copper plate script on its cover, and marbled end-papers; a quality handout of the time. There is also a copper printing block featuring a drawing of a circa 1910 Rothwell touring car and probably used in newspaper advertise-ments, and a saddle-mounted cycle toolbag with the name 'Rothwell' embossed on the flap in bold capitals. To date, no Eclipse knitting machine has come to light, but this same family collection does include the medal awarded in 1879 by Oldham Agricultural Society (estab-lished in 1874) to Shepherd, Rothwell & Hough for their collection of sewing machines, illustrated in Chapter 2.

St Andrew's, the Oldham church where the Leyland windows commemorating Fred Rothwell had been installed, had become redundant as the surrounding former residential area was cleared for redevelopment, and it was demolished in 1982. At that time, Julie Dawson's father, Hartley, had saved the brass plaque that had been in place below the windows and that recorded this memorial and its dedication. Intrigued by photographs taken of the windows by her father, Julie determined to try to discover whether the church fittings had been saved, and if so, where they might have gone. The then Vicar of Delph, the Rev John Brocklehurst, told her that Manchester Central Reference Library held all the records of closed churches. Together, they investigated and discovered the name of Hardmans, a Birmingham firm that had bought the contents, fittings and also the windows from St Andrews. After numerous setbacks and vicissitudes, and commendable persistence on her part, what remained of the windows first was located, still with a tattered identifying label attached, and then acquired by Julie. Parts of each of the pair had been either used to repair other stained glass windows, or lost, but, with some work, sufficient remained for one pair of panels to be recreated. By the happiest of chances, a pair of windows adjacent to the

From transparencies taken by Hartley Schofield in 1982, the two pairs of windows commemorating Fred Rothwell's life are seen in their original location in St Andrew's Church, Oldham. Left – Jesus bids the fishermen become 'fishers of men'; right – the raising of Lazarus from the Dead.

font in St Thomas's Church in Delph, in contrast to the other stained glass windows along that same side, had always contained plain obscured glass… and the dimensions matched exactly. After further delays, and obtaining the necessary permissions, John Brocklehurst was finally able to re-dedicate the transplanted windows in St Thomas's very shortly before he left for another parish. Rothwell and Schofield family members were present on that occasion, and a matching plaque and the old one from St Andrews are fixed below the Fred Rothwell memorial windows in their new and appropriate setting.

From the sewing machine era of Messrs. Shepherd, Rothwell & Hough, surviving Eclipse machines are not particularly uncommon, although they are found in far smaller numbers than those of the main makers, Singer and Jones, whose machines spread across the globe. Bradbury sewing machines too are relatively widespread, especially in the Oldham area, implying that a high proportion of their sales had been made locally. In fact, the Curator at Gallery Oldham, Sean Baggaley, says that scarcely a month goes by without his being offered at least one ancient sewing machine, usually a Bradbury and more rarely an Eclipse, and unless the offer is that of an example outstanding in some way, these gestures have to be tactfully declined. In store, the Museum has a considerable number of different types of Bradbury sewing machines and a couple of

The remaining portions of the windows installed and dedicated in St Thomas's Church, Delph, in 2008. Rothwell and Schofield family members, with, at the front, the Rev John Brocklehurst, Mrs Marion Schofield (Hartley's widow), and her daughter, Julie Dawson.

Julie Dawson's SR&H treadle machine is complete with steel dressmaking pins, reels of cotton and contemporary accessories.

treadle Eclipse models. From time to time, items from the stores are included in exhibitions staged to mark Oldham's industrial past. Julie Dawson has a superb treadle Eclipse sewing machine that is kept company by a small Shepherd, Rothwell & Hough hand-operated table model.

Neither Shepherd, Rothwell & Hough's nor the Eclipse name appears on any known and surviving tram conductors' bell punches, although it has frequently been mentioned that the famous firm of Ashton-under-Lyne, Williamsons, did have such an arrangement with Rothwells for their manufacture of parts, and possibly the whole machines. Collectors have several of these bell punches, and a typical example can be seen on display in the Portland Basin Museum in Ashton.

Rothwell cycles feature prominently in the cycling press up to the early 1900s, and receipts survive for their sale, and likewise they appear in period photographs of competition cyclists, where the captions are eager to publicise the makes of cycle on which

The maker's plate from the Benz car imported by the Rothwell brothers in 1897.

A Rothwell cycle toolbag, as attached to the saddle.

Above – wheels with wood rims and minimal equipment are features of the fixed gear Rothwell path racer, made circa 1902.

Left – this racing machine offers minimal wind resistence.

race successes had been achieved. The familiar need to repaint an old and much-used bicycle has resulted in the transfers that revealed the maker's identity disappearing over the years, and many are the old bicycles treasured by collectors and enthusiasts where evidence of the make has been lost this way. Some cycles can be identified by details of the design of the crowns of the front forks or other prominent features, and some makers adopted special designs of chainwheel spoking patterns that were specific to their own machines. Study of the only known remaining Rothwell bicycle shows fork crowns lacking any such unusual identification features. The chainwheel of this cycle features a six-pointed star pattern of spokes, and this is quite unlike the chainwheels seen in the motorcycle adverts of 1903-04. The surviving bicycle is displayed in the Saddleworth Museum at Uppermill, a few miles north east of Oldham, and belongs to Julie Dawson, great granddaughter of Fred Rothwell. It is a gents' path racer of circa 1902, and has dropped handlebars, no brakes, a fixed gear and 26 x 1¼ ins one-piece Kundtz wooden rims to its wheels. It is in remarkable condition, with the original finish and transfers intact. As racing machines had a specialised use, and keen competitors always sought the latest developments, outdated machines were soon discarded and their survival has been far less likely than that of an everyday bicycle. Early racing bicycles are extremely rare items.

The motorcycle mentioned in Chapter 3 belongs to Messrs Wildes of Leeds, long established dealers in new and older motorcycles, and true enthusiasts for two-wheeled machines. It is claimed to be of 1902 manufacture, and has an early pattern of 1¼hp Minerva 'clip on' engine. There's an unconfirmed rumour of another survivor, also in Yorkshire.

Above – offside view of the motorcycle described in the text; and – left – detail photographs of its 1¼hp Minerva engine.

The Wildes' machine still presents generally in good condition, and has the appearance of an 'older restoration' which subsequently has seen little if any use, and shows some very light surface deterioration compatible with long term museum storage. It was purchased in 1967 from an enthusiast and collector of early motorcycles in Halifax, along with a couple of other machines. Records suggest that it was registered BHD101 in 1955, a Dewsbury CBC series and presumably issued at the time when it was taxed for road use on completion of restoration. The engine number is unknown (although a Vintage Motorcycle Club record quotes '195'), and the frame number is recorded as 24843. As would be expected of such an early machine, the frame differs little from those of 'commercial' pedal bicycles as used by butchers, bakers and postmen. The bottom bracket carrying the pedals and chainwheel is clearly an early pattern, and has an unusual design feature in that the crank pin is mounted eccentrically within the bracket, allowing chain tension to be adjusted by rotating its locating bush. The wheel hubs are period and are in their original nickel finish, but the rims appear to date from more recent times. The front wheel is unbraked, yet period illustrations show stirrup-pattern front brakes. The handlebars are made from rather wide-bore tubing, and are narrow in span: the handgrip (one is missing) is made of horn. A cycle-pattern Lucas 'King of the Road' nickel-plated oil lamp is fitted.

As with most primitive contemporary motorcycles, it has no clutch and only a single speed. The Minerva engine of this survivor has an automatic overhead inlet valve and

As they are today – Wilton Place, 10 Edward Street (left), Fred and Frances Rothwell's home; and (right) Stoneswood, Delph, Tom Rothwell's family home from 1906 to 1918.

side-placed exhaust valve. The carburettor cannot be the correct one, as it incorporates a water jacket with threaded unions, and would originally have been fitted to a water-cooled engine. The triangular exhaust box is old and genuine, and is mounted immediately below the fuel tank, this to assist vaporization of the fuel for the surface-type carburettor that originally would have been fitted. Brammer belting drive runs from the crankshaft pulley to a belt rim attached to the rear wheel. The rear part of the fuel tank assembly has an offside door, which opens, by removing upwards a brass rod, to reveal the space where the trembler coil and dry batteries would have been located. The tank has been repainted a deep green. The Rothwell badge, with the 'garter' surrounding the capital letter 'R', has been carefully hand-touched in on both sides of the tank, possibly over the original. Behind the seat tube is a cylindrical oil tank with plunger pump and pipework leading into the crankcase. Period illustrations do not show this feature; instead the hand pump for oil was an external fitting to a compartment of the main tank body, in which the oil supply was stored.

Tom Rothwell's last home, Stoneswood, in Delph, is a magnificent late Victorian residence, a mansion standing in extensive grounds. Internally, much of the original elaborate period woodwork and ceilings remain. Today it is a care home for the elderly, well-maintained and the owners respect its architectural importance. Fred and Frances' last home, Wilton Place, 10 Edward Street, also still stands and is in sound

The site of Matley's Buildings on the corner of Union Street and Gas Street (the latter renamed Rhodes Bank), and occupied by the fine premises of Messrs. Hirst, Kidd & Rennie, publishers of the Oldham Chronicle.

Left – an artist's 'creative' impression of the Viscount Street factory, from the 1907 Rothwell car sales catalogue; and, below – more prosaic reality – the works captured by the camera in 1963. Bottom – the site of Viscount Street and of the Eclipse Machine Company's works now lie beneath the Grange Arts Centre and the campus of Oldham College.

condition. A substantial brick built double-fronted semi-detached town house built circa 1860, it is now used by Oldham MBC Social Services Department.

Messrs. Shepherd, Rothwell & Hough's first works was located at Matley's Buildings, a few hundred yards west of Mumps railway bridge. Vacated when the firm moved to Viscount Street in 1881, later occupants of these premises were Messrs. Hirst Kidd & Rennie, printers and publishers of the *Oldham Chronicle*. This same firm still occupies the site today, but in a fine new building constructed around 25 years ago.

The Eclipse Machine Company's 'new Sewing Machine Works' in Viscount Street was later used for many years as a bakery by the Co-operative Wholesale Society, but now the old factory site and indeed the street itself have disappeared in the redevelopment of the town. Today, Grange Arts Centre and the Sports Hall of Oldham College and the surrounding campus and car parks occupy the area where once stood the Rothwell works on the western, downhill side of Viscount Street.

Only one Rothwell car has ever come to light, a 20hp Model A of 1910, and the story of this vehicle deserves a chapter to itself.

9. The Surviving 1910 20hp Rothwell Car

Still with the only Rothwell car believed to exist is the original motor vehicle registration entry paperwork that was handed to the first owner on 9 May 1911. It is yellowed with age, and where it has been folded, the creases have worn through, and attempts to repair it with adhesive tape in the long-distant past have added further to its discolouration. But it records that CP215 was issued by the County Borough of Halifax to William Greenwood of Thornleigh, Parkinson Lane, in that same town: a 20hp Rothwell pleasure car designated for 'Private' use. The entry recording its colour is hard to read, but can just be made out as

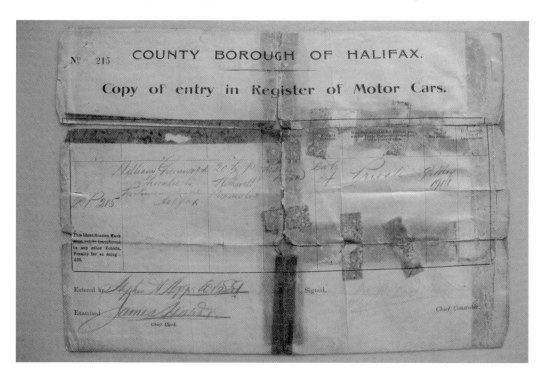

'reddish brown', and 'weight unladen' was entered as 'Cwts 24'. The previous year, Mr Greenwood had registered (on 13 July) a 20hp Rothwell van CP178, so he must have been favourably impressed by the make to place this further order for a private car.

The census of 1911 is now available, and it confirms Mr Greenwood's residence at the Parkinson Lane address with his wife, three sons and two daughters, aged between 25 and 10, and a servant. He was employed as a stores manager in a 'distributive business', the census of ten years earlier stating that at that time he was a

'Thornleigh', 32 Parkinson Lane, Halifax, in 2009 – William Greenwood's former home is the left hand house of the pair.

self-employed grocer, as indeed he had been in 1891, at a previous address, 11 Kingsley Place. His age in 1911 is given as 51.

Access to the garage behind 'Thornleigh', occupied by Greenwood's Rothwell CP215 from 1911 to 1943.

'Thornleigh', 32 Parkinson Lane stands yet, lightly modernised and still the substantial family home it was a century ago. Semi detached, three storeyed and built of the same local stone as are all the nearby houses of similar age and type, it has a short rising front garden with footpath leading from a gate up to the front door, a garden or yard to the rear with a high wall separating it from Holly Grove, the street that runs up the side of 'Thornleigh.' In this side wall, distant from the house, are set the doors that give access to the garage. 'Thornleigh' is entirely typical of the kind of home in which a comfortably-off middle class family of Edwardian northern England might be expected to have lived.

Those involved with the car in the early 1960s were told that Mr Greenwood used the Rothwell until Lloyd George introduced his horsepower tax in 1920, and then, in disgust at what he considered punitive taxation, he laid up the car. This new Act introduced the Road Fund, the income from which was intended to pay for remedial work on the roads resulting from the lack of maintenance during the war years. Successive governments have been happy to find additional applications! The effect was to quadruple existing vehicle taxation levels from 1921. Verification of this anecdote is confirmed by a letter on file from the Motor Vehicle Registration Dept of the County Borough of Halifax. They wrote in 1965 to state that CP251 was never licensed or any change of ownership registered after the introduction of Roads Act, 1920. Many years later, domestic fuel shortages led to the bodywork being 'chopped up' for use as firewood, this despite the pleadings of local car enthusiasts to

the owner, at least to preserve intact the long-stored car even if he remained steadfast in his refusals to sell it. By the existence of outrigger brackets fixed to the chassis side rails to carry a wider body, and metal uprights, all seen in 1960s photographs of the chassis, allied to the long wheelbase and platform rear springing, an informed guess is that originally this car carried landaulette coachwork.

The landaulette was an expensive, formal style of coachwork where the rear compartment had a fixed roof and side window frames, and yet could be opened by collapsing a leather hood. The driver's seat was separate, in front of a division, more commonly with a roof but with open sides to his compartment. An elaborate body of this type would provide considerably more firewood than an open touring body!

A subsequent owner, Mr Ronald S Kemlo wrote in 1962 that he had

Photographs taken in 1962 of the Rothwell chassis at Mr Kemlo's home in Sheffield, on the day Hartley Schofield collected his new acquisition. Left to right – Geoff Ashton; Serge Korochenko; Dr Braddock (an interested friend); Hartley; mechanics Eric Houseman and Michael Mott.

The engine was intact but the steering column was detached from the steering box – some but not all of the steering parts were to hand. Below: Mr Kemlo is busy at the front of the chassis: the drip feed oilers can be seen on the dash, as can the speedometer drive from the propeller shaft.

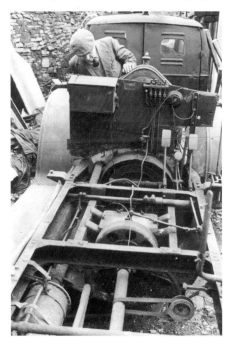

purchased the Rothwell from William Greenwood: since Greenwood died aged 81 in 1943, Kemlo too must have owned the car for 20 years or more. He also wrote that circumstances had prevented him carrying out the reconditioning and other restoration work that he planned on purchase of the car. Another Sheffield man, P J Wilson of Dransfield Road, Crosspool, enquired in the press and wrote to the Montagu Motor Museum (now the National Motor Museum) in the late 1950s, searching for information about Rothwell cars. It is unclear whether he was enquiring on Kemlo's behalf, or on this own, possibly hopeful of acquiring the car himself. From such evidence as is available, it seems most likely that Kemlo's account is correct in that he himself purchased it direct from William Greenwood. Wilson's appeals in Oldham's local press must have alerted Hartley Schofield to the existence of the sole remaining Rothwell car and opened the way for him to purchase it.

Greatly spurred by the popular success of the film, 'Genevieve' (1953), interest in veteran cars had blossomed. Although decrepit, the Rothwell had been stored under cover out of the rain, and remained basically sound, with only surface rust on the chassis parts. By 1943, all the bodywork had gone, as had the bonnet: the mudguards remained but only the nearside running board. The steering wheel, with the levers and quadrants for control of ignition and throttle and the outer casing of the steering column too had disappeared. Rock hard, white rubber 'grooved' tyres remained on a couple of wheel rims.

At that time, the establishment of firms equipped to undertake the restoration of incomplete early cars was some years in the future, and the only options available to someone faced with a bodyless early car chassis were either to locate a more or less suitable body from another car of similar age, and adapt it to fit, or to make one from scratch themselves to the best of their ability. Mr Kemlo came to realise that, for him, this was an insuperable obstacle.

Now, as aforementioned, Hartley Schofield (hence Hartley), the father of Julie Dawson, was a grandson of Fred Rothwell. His mother, Clara, was Fred's second daughter. Hartley and Edward Megson, his business partner, ran Messrs H. Hughes & Bolton Ltd, Rootes Group agents in Oldham, and he had a lifelong passion for cars and for motor sport. A motor trader since the textile slump of 1930, Hartley had owned a number of interesting cars and had travelled to Belfast to watch every pre-war Ulster TT held. This road race, held over 30 laps of the 13·4-mile Ards circuit, was run from 1928 to 1936 inclusive. He competed in a Jowett Javelin in the Monte Carlo Rallies of 1949 and 1950, and knew many of the personalities from the motor sporting world. Anything connected with the early days of motoring in the Oldham area interested him, and of course he always felt great pride in his direct connection with the Rothwell family's products.

Hartley purchased the Rothwell chassis from Mr Kemlo in November 1962, and installed it in the top floor workshop at H. Hughes & Bolton, which was accessed by a lift.

William Boddy, celebrated Editor of *Motor Sport* magazine,

Back in H. Hughes & Bolton's premises in Oldham, dismantling is under way. Top left is seen the ignition trembler coil box, centrally, the vaned fan clamped round the outside of the flywheel, and lower left the transmission brake drum.

The rear axle has been removed, and the 'platform' rear suspension is revealed – the transverse leaf spring is shackled to the rear ends of familiar semi-elliptical rear springs. Outrigger brackets for a wider body can be seen attached to the chassis side rails. Serge Korochenko, the Polish mechanic, to the left.

was but one of many interested parties who made their way to the garage premises to inspect this unique piece of motoring history, and the June 1963 issue of that highly-regarded magazine carried his article on Rothwell cars and this example in particular, as an instalment in the periodical's long-running series, 'Fragments on Forgotten Makes'.

Earlier, and following on from a local newspaper article about the Rothwell, this book's author, as a callow youth had also come to pay his respects, and wrote in his diary as follows:

'… the back axle has been done. But nothing else other than dismantling.… It is in good condition on the whole, a little rust… but there's a horrible old repair to the chassis side member on the nearside by the engine.' Then, after some notes about the technical features of the chassis that repeat those described in Chapter 5, '…original paint and lining, red-brown and black, remains on the wheels and springs. Massive finned tube radiator…' These notes concluded, 'What a car!'

That same major difficulty, the absence of any bodywork, so essential to the project, eventually brought home to Hartley the magnitude of the commitment confronting his aim of achieving an authentic restoration of the Rothwell. Running his business left little spare time to advance matters himself, the chassis was taking up space needed for profitable day-to-day repair work on customers' vehicles, and it was bad business economics to divert the mechanics on his staff to work on the Rothwell whilst routine work was held up. So, two years after purchasing the car, he was happy to sell it on, principally because the man who was to purchase it, Peter Stott, a member of a prominent Oldham family and already an established and active old car enthusiast, had the means, contacts and a similarly strong interest in the Rothwell's local origins to carry the restoration through to a proper completion.

Enterprising firms specialising in repair and restoration work on early cars were just beginning to emerge in the mid-1960s. Some grew from the enthusiasm of practical vintage car owners who started by undertaking work for others, from which point came the need to find suitable premises, and expansion by taking on additional skilled workers. Others, such as I Wilkinson & Son Ltd of Derby, are old-established firms that saw the opportunity to extend their activities into a field beginning to become viable through the growing appreciation for and increasing values of old motorcars.

Above – the framework for the new body on the restored chassis is completed at I Wilkinson & Son in Derby in 1967.

Below – work has progressed further: the panelling is done, windscreen framework and the running boards are under way.

Wilkinsons have a long history going back to the early years of the 20th century when the firm, initially blacksmiths, went on to build bodies first for horse-drawn, then powered vehicles. A director of Wilkinsons, Frank Gilbert, was, and is, an enthusiast for vintage Alvis 12/50 cars and the ultra-sporting 'duck's back' style of 12/50 body, usually finished in bare polished aluminium, was relatively simple to reproduce. Frank owned an excellent original example, which therefore was available to be copied, and the

first of what grew to a considerable number, maybe 30, of these bodies started to emerge from the Derby workshops. The nature of the construction of cars of the 1920s and into the 1930s, when separate chassis and bodies were the norm, led to many cars, especially hard-used sports models, reaching a state where the original bodies had deteriorated to a far greater extent than had the chassis and engine. The mechanics of these cars were more straightforward and cost less to recondition and repair than did their coachwork. The success of the 'Wilkinson' Alvis bodies led to increasing amounts of similar work coming to the firm, and in the autumn of 1966, they were engaged to build a copy of one of the styles of open touring bodies illustrated in a sales catalogue on the Rothwell chassis. Prior to this, everything on the Rothwell's chassis had been checked over and refurbished as necessary by Michael Fitton, a practical engineer and a colleague of Peter Stott.

Only the headlamp brackets remain to be refitted, as the finished car, varnish gleaming, stands outside Wilkinsons' premises.

Less than 12 months later, Wilkinsons' work was complete, and the car then was seen out on a few occasions and at some events. Thereafter, lack of time and the pressure of other commitments forced the Rothwell once more to slumber in storage, but happily now safe, dry and intact. It changed hands once again in November 2008, when purchased by Julie Dawson, whom, it would appear, has the distinction of being only its fifth owner in 99 years.

Since this recent change of ownership, work on the car has been directed at completing the few unfinished details. For instance, there were no side or rear lamps or brackets for them, and the trembler coil ignition system needed specialist restoration. The magneto was overhauled, and the steering column refurbishment carried out long ago have been made more satisfactory. A steering wheel of the correct period was located and also a set of the hand levers to control the ignition timing and throttle opening that pass down the centre of the steering column. No spare

The 1910 Rothwell made a rare appearance at a concours d'elegance at the VSCC race meeting at Oulton Park in the 1970s.

2008 views – the offside view shows the HT system prominent, with Simms magneto and one of the two sets of sparking plugs. Separate cylinder blocks, non-detachable cylinder heads and an inspection plate in the crankcase all are curious features to modern eyes.

The nearside view of the engine shows the push rods for the overhead inlet valve gear and trembler coil ignition to the second set of sparking plugs.

Undoing the single large nut releases the inlet valves and their cages – to the left, the cage complete, and to the right, the valve assembly remains in its seating once its retaining cover is removed.

wheel was present, and a Stepney pattern spare rim and tyre have been built up from period parts. Hopefully, the car will be run again very shortly; and then, to mark its centenary year, Julie Dawson plans to follow in her own Rothwell car the route taken by her forebears in a more primitive Rothwell back in 1904, as mentioned in Chapter 4 and detailed in Appendix 3.

Turning now to the car itself, the initial reaction on confronting the Rothwell is that it has a real and imposing presence. Its lengthy wheelbase and high build certainly bracket it with larger types of car of the same age. The chassis detail and radiator are robust and functional, and eschew any delicate

Recent work has enhanced the only remaining Rothwell car. April 2010 witnessed glorious spring sunshine, and the car looks at its best in its centenary year.

or elegant touches. In every way the car is a typically northern, no-nonsense product; one designed to stand up to unlimited hard usage. The overhead inlet valve arrangement results in a tall engine and therefore bonnet and radiator, and the confident and substantial approach to engine design is equally apparent in the large steering box and the gearbox.

Cycle threads are an unexpected feature of many of the nuts and studs on the engine and chassis, a legacy from its maker's background. Unusual too are the steering connections, whereby the drag link operates a bell crank arm, pivoted from the offside steering arm, and the track rod linking offside and nearside steering arms is placed forward of the axle. This forward-positioned track rod is a feature found commonly in car designs earlier than that of the Rothwell, but the few other important makes that also perpetuated this feature included Napier and Panhard-Levassor. The rear hubs also have a heavy design. Instrumentation for the driver is confined to a speedometer, reading from zero to 60 mph, driven by a flat belt from a pulley on the open propeller shaft, plus the four sight feeds for the lubrication system, as mentioned earlier.

Although the body is recent, the brasswork of the windscreen frame is of period Auster make, and a Boa Constrictor bulb horn is a striking feature. A period lighting set has been gathered together, with Lucas no. 676 11-inch diameter acetylene headlights supplied with

gas from a running-board mounted generator, paraffin-burning side lamps of similar age and a pair of steel 'Dependance' rear lamps also lit by paraffin. A coach-painted finish in dark Brunswick green, the colour most frequently chosen for Rothwells according to the evidence of the Oldham registration records, is set off by the chassis and wheels being finished in dark red, lined out in black, and the mudguards are in black enamel.

Two established dates bracket the precise time that this particular car left the Rothwell factory. The offside top of the crankcase carries the date stamp JULY 25 10, adjacent to an inspector's mark. Five other aluminium castings under the bonnet also bear other July 1910 dates. Secondly, CP215 was issued on 9 May 1911, when the car was registered for use on the roads. Following factory inspection of a new component such as the crankcase, it could rest for a length of time that might vary anything between hours and months before it was incorporated into an engine and then a chassis, and before that in turn was assembled into a complete vehicle. Another imponderable is whether a body for a specific chassis was being built as the chassis was assembled, or whether the chassis was completed before the coachwork was begun. In the case of a chassis that had been arranged to go to an outside coachbuilder, then the latter would almost certainly be the case. Elaborate bodies took much longer to build, trim and coachpaint than the simplest types. And whilst many customers could wait for their bespoke orders to be completed, another car could be built 'on spec' and remain in a dealer's showroom for weeks or even months. The Dating Committee of the Veteran Car Club of Great Britain researched this

The lengthy wheelbase is apparent in this side view.

Rothwell in 1968, and decided that 1910 was the most likely year of its construction, and such subsequent evidence that has been discovered does not challenge that decision.

The specification of this car closely tallies with that published in the sales catalogue issued for the 1910 season (and therefore probably illustrating features existing in 1909), with a few exceptions. One variation is that the engine crankcase photographs show twin inspection hatches on the nearside, whilst this surviving car has a single one on the offside. Further, the catalogue gives track options as 4ft 3in for the cheaper Model 'B' and 4ft 8ins for the Model 'A': the track of CP215 is 4ft 4ins. The wheelbase of the Model 'A' was 9ft 9ins, and the 'B', 9ft 6ins. CP215 measures 9ft 8ins. Tyre sizes quoted are 815 x 105 all round on the cheaper Model 'B', and 870 x 90 front and 880 x 120 rear on the 'A', but CP215 has 820 x 120 rims and tyres all round and these rims would certainly appear never to have been changed. The 1910 catalogue also illustrates the Mulliner staggered spoke wheels in two line drawings, but these could be outdated printing blocks reused. The 1910 catalogue is the closest reference source, and on comparison with the illustrations therein, CP215 has front and rear axle features, wheel hub configuration, spring hangers, side lever quadrant type and chassis side rail rivetting patterns that all match the Model 'B' and differ from the 'A'. The conclusion is that CP215 is a longer wheelbase version of the Model 'B', and was made late in 1910.

Inconsistencies of this kind seem unthinkable today, but in those days of more or less individual construction in small numbers, relatively major changes were made easily in the light of customer request, necessity or experimentation. Those were times of rapid development, and variations between catalogue specifications and the vehicles that subsequently

Above – there's not much protection for the driver and front seat passenger, other than the windscreen. But the view of the road ahead could not be bettered!

Right – the 1910 20hp Rothwell is poised ready to embark on its second century.

emerged from the factory were not at all uncommon. Most likely the discrepancies arose as changes were made during the course of the production year. These alterations then would find their way into the catalogues – if at all – for the following season.

10. Closing Thoughts

A recurring regret has been that the task of assembling this information was not undertaken earlier. In particular, Hartley Schofield would have known personally many of the people mentioned in these pages, and his wide range of local contacts, men of his own age or even older, also would have been able to confirm details and provide information at which now we can only make informed guesses. Family members now deceased could have given us a much fuller human assessment of many of those involved with the doings in Viscount Street. We have been unable to discover anything about the internal layout of the Rothwell factory or its equipment and facilities, or the size of its workforce.

The successful local businessmen of the Edwardian age supported each other. During the preparation of this book, the names of a number of these local families have been revealed as customers for Rothwell cars. The first purchase recorded by a lady was that of a dark green 20hp car by Mrs Emily Bradbury of The Grange, Uppermill in June 1908. She is thought to have had no connection with the sewing machine and motorcycle Bradburys and that her family had woollen mills. As well as Dronsfields purchasing Rothwell lorries, James Dronsfield also bought a 1910 Rothwell limousine BU240 for his personal use. Likewise, Samuel Megson of Oak Leather Works bought both lorries and private cars from Rothwells. In addition to being general curriers, this firm specialised in drive belting for machinery, and their works was in Connaught Street. George Ingham, who had two private cars, and his business, the Oldham Rope & Twine Company, were customers, as was Oldham Corporation. Yet another example was Mr Buckley of the leading local department store, Messrs Buckley & Prockter. Dr Fawsitt was a prominent physician and surgeon in Oldham who purchased two Rothwell 20hp tourers, replacing his 1907 model BU105 with a similar car, BU344 in May 1912, and William Moseley who bought one of the early 6hp Rothwells (BU24) was a well-known Oldham dentist.

John Murgatroyd, closely involved with the Rothwell brothers, was a director of Richmond Mill, Hollinwood, a large cotton spinning factory. Other local firms buying Rothwell vehicles in those days included Pollards the newsagents; textile machinery makers and exporters Samuel Dodd & Sons of Lyon Works in Tattershall Street, Werneth; Jonathan Partington & Son, and Alfred Ferguson & Co of Hollinwood. Charles Bullough, the confectioner of Yorkshire Street bought a bought BU117 (probably) a 20hp touring car in 1907, and John Farrow, a coach and cab operator of Manchester Street, a 20hp landaulette, perhaps for his business, early in 1909.

The material and information that has been preserved in the family, with additional research, and the assistance of so many well-wishers has nevertheless resulted in relevant material of adequate quality and quantity to make what it is hoped is a reasonably accurate and interesting account. It is astonishing that from some hundreds of Rothwell motor vehicles that left Viscount Street, only one car still exists as a testament to this local enterprise. But how fortunate we are to have that one as, already decrepit by 1940, its chances of prolonged survival at that time must have seemed very poor.

The final impression is one of respect for the Rothwell brothers and their families – that they were inspired, and capable of achieving their ambitious objective, of sustaining their position for some years, and maybe also that they were perceptive in their assessment: that, after 1918, small provincial motor manufacturers would have no lasting place in a radically changed world.

Appendix 1

Recorded Rothwell cars and motorcycles, information culled from various registration and other sources. Whilst it is accepted that many more such entries remain undiscovered or lost forever, this existing data gives us the best available evidence of production figures and dates of currency for the various models of motorcycle and car sold under the Rothwell name. Some entries in old registration records do not include the body type fitted, or are incomplete in other ways. As registrations were introduced in December 1903, some of the earliest entries were issued to vehicles manufactured at various lengths of time before that date.

Photographs exist of several cars which are side views, and therefore cannot be identified from a registration number. They may or may not be included in the following list and are not included in the total number of recorded Rothwell vehicles.

They are listed in date order of registration mark and number issue, with very brief details and the source of the information shown by the following codes:

David Hales's archives	= DAH
Gowan Coulthard	= RGC
Oldham CBC registration records	= Ol
Rochdale CBC registration records	= Ro
Manx vehicle registrations listing, 1914	= IoM
De Dion Bouton engine	= DDB
Where the body colour is contrastingly lined out	= /
Hood and windscreen	= h&s
Photographic evidence of this vehicle exists	= *P*
Tame Valley Tin Works, Dukinfield	= TVTW
Reissued registration	= *

Motorcycles

Date	Horsepower	Regn	First owner and location	Source	Comments
Dec 6 '03	-	CA10	H D M Jones, Wrexham	DAH	
Jan 1 '04	-	CK97	J Reed, Deepdale, Preston	DAH	
Jan 5 '04	2¾	W135	H Whitehead, Sheffield	DAH	Whitley engine
Jan 11 '04	-	MS52	J K Shanks, Denny, Stirling	DAH	'motorcycle & forecar'
Jan 21 '04	1½	W170	J D Brian, Sheffield	DAH	Minerva engine
Feb 29 '04	-	FM41	J Stubbs, Tarporley	DAH	
Feb 10 '04	-	M338	J Gibson, Crewe	DAH	
Jul 11 '04	3	M562	W Ruscoe, Kelsall, Cheshire	DAH	
Jul 25 '05	1¾	EN56	J Ayrton, Bury	DAH	

Cars and commercial vehicles

Date	Horsepower	Regn	First owner and location	Source	Comments
Dec 31 '03	6 DDB	BU11	J Barrett, Junction Inn, Oldham	Ol	'oak varnished'
Jan 1 '04	9	M208	J Conneely, Nantwich	DAH	tonneau, cardinal/black
Jan 5 '04	6	AM213	A Bathurst Brown, Salisbury	DAH	2-str, blue
Jan 21 '04	12	BU15	Eclipse M Co > S Dodd, Oldham	Ol	tonneau, dk green/yellow
Mar 19 '04	6 DDB	BU21	J Barrett, Junction Inn	Ol	green, yellow wheels
May 4 '04	6	BU23	R Hamer, Barlow St, Oldham	Ol	red
May 5 '04	6	AX93	W Murphy, Cwmbran	DAH	2-str, dark red
? mid '04	10/12?	B330	(unknown)	P	tonneau
Jun 7 '04	6	M519	J Bailey, Stalybridge	DAH	2-str + spider, sage green/red
Jun 9 '04	6	BU24	Wm Moseley, Oldham	Ol	green
Jun 10 '04	12	BU25	S Dodd & Sons, Oldham	Ol	dk green; yellow wheels
Jun 11 '04	12	BU26	J Cowper, Union St West, Oldham	Ol	green: red later
Jun 18 '04	12	BU28	J Prestwich, Middleton Rd, Oldham	Ol	red/black
Jun 20 '04	6	BU29	E Robinson, Dobcross	Ol; P	2-str; green
Sep 19 '04	12	BU35	E & G Pollard, Langley St, Oldham	Ol	dog cart; 16cwt; green
Nov 1 '04	12	BU37	Fred Rothwell, 10 Edward St	Ol	tonneau, green, red wheels
early '05	10-12	K371	(unknown)	P	swing seat tonneau, light colour
Jul 24 '05	10-12	BU49	J Stuttard, Windsor Rd, Oldham	Ol; P	4-str; cream/red
Aug 8 '05	12	BU50	John Murgatroyd, Frederick St	Ol	4-str; green/red
Aug 11 '05	10-12	BU51	E Robinson, Dobcross	Ol	tonneau, red/black
Jan 22 '06	12	BU57	Dronsfields, Atlas Wks	Ol	cart, maroon, gold letters
Feb 9 '06	10-12	AX137	W Murphy, Cwmbran	DAH	green/dark red
Feb 15 '06	24	BU58	J Murgatroyd, Stoneswood, Delph	Ol	motor brougham, dk gn
Feb 17 '06	20	EN81	J Entwistle, Bury	DAH	'flex sided body', grey
Apr 17 '06	6	BU68	W Pardoe, Middleton	Ol	2-str; red
May 3 '06	12	M1196	G H Smith, Knutsford	DAH	tonneau, dark green
May 3 '06	12	M1197	J Grice, Knutsford	DAH	tourer, dark blue
May 8 '06	12	BU70	Dronsfields, Atlas Wks	Ol	cart; blue/red, gold letters
May 15 '06	20	BU71	J Murgatroyd > Tom Rothwell	Ol P	5-str; dark green
May 26 '06	12	BU75	R Thatcher, Honeywell Lane	Ol P	side entrance 4-str, dk red; 2cyl Aster engine
Jun 6 '06	12-14	*BU77	J Sucksmith, Milnrow Rd, Oldham	Ol	tonneau, red
Jul 10 '06	12	BU80	R Downes, Union St, Oldham	Ol	side entrance, blue
Aug 14 '06	20-24	BU83	Saml Dronsfield, Windsor Rd	Ol	dk green, red wheels
Sep 10 '06	12	BU87	Wm Robinson, Wellington Rd	Ol	cab, dk green/black
Nov 20 '06	10-12	CA211	J Pierce, Abergele	DAH	tonneau, cream
Dec 21 '06	10	BU91	Eclipse Machine Co	Ol	delivery van, black/green
Mar 29 '07	8	BU102	E Atkinson, Corporation St	Ol	tonneau, dk red, cape hood

Date	*Horsepower*	*Regn*	*First owner and location*	*Source*	*Comments*
Apr 25 '07	20	BU105	Thos Fawsitt MRCS, Union St	Ol	5-str; dk green/white
May 1 '07	12-14	M1577	H Stephens, Leatherhead	DAH	landaulette, blue/red
May 13 '07	24	BU107	Eclipse > J Dronsfield	Ol	open 5-str; grey
Jun 6 '07	12	BU109	John Manwood, TVTW	Ol	cart, green, gold letters
Jun 20 '07	12-14	BU111	Jonathan Partington & Son	Ol	dk green, red upholstery
(?) Jul '07	12-14	LN5856	(unknown)	P	side entrance 4-str, White & Poppe engine
Jul 10 '07	20	BU112	Eclipse Machine Co	Ol	side ent. tonneau, green
Jul 17 '07	12-14	BU113	John Sutcliffe, Savoy St, Oldham	Ol	red/white
Jul 20 '07	12-14	BU114	Dronsfields, Atlas Wks	Ol	deliv cart, dk green/gold
Nov 5 '07	18	BU117	Chas Bullough, Yorkshire St	Ol	side ent, dark green
Nov 8 '07	20-24	BU119	Thos Bates, Lamb Inn, Oldham	Ol P	side ent, green, hood
Nov 11 '07	15	BU120	E Robinson, Parkside, G/field	Ol	side ent, dark green
Jan 9 '08	12-14	BU122	Johnson, Clapham & Morris	Ol	black & green, lettered
Feb 25 '08	20	BU128	John Marcroft, Belgrave Rd	Ol	green/black
Mar 31 '08	12-14	BU133	Daniel Garforth, Failsworth	Ol	4-str, green/red
Apr 8 '08	20	BU136	George Ingham, Queens Rd	Ol P	dk green, green upholstery
Jun 19 '08	20-25	BU147	Emily Bradbury, Uppermill	Ol	dk green/white
Jun 30 '08	20	BU151	Platt Bros, Hartford Wks	Ol	landaulette, green
Jan 4 '09	6	BU159	Jas Porter, Shaw Rd, Oldham	Ol	dark green, yellow wheels
Jan 14 '09	20	BU162	Eclipse. (F Bradley in 3/09)	Ol	side entrance, green
Mar 1 '09	20-25	BU168	John Farrow, Manchester St	Ol	landaulette, green/black
Mar 18 '09	20	BU171	Oak Leather Wks, Cross Bank	Ol	lorry
Apr 23 '09	20	BU175	Fred Mayall, 38 Pitt St, Oldham	Ol	tourer, dark green
May 12 '09	20	BU181	Chas Hardman, Queens Rd	Ol	2-str, French grey
May 25 '09	20	BU184	Joshua Megson, Belgrave Rd	Ol	side entrance, green
Jun 9 '09	14	BU186	Hardman, Ingham & Dawson	Ol	25cwt lory, dark red
Jun 29 '09	10-12	BU187	Wm Pardoe, The Theatre, M/n	Ol	2-str, cream
Jul 1 '09	20	BU188	Oldham Rope & Twine Co	Ol	landaulette, dark green
Jul 2 '09	10-12	BU190	Wm Norton, 117 Villa Rd, Oldham	Ol	2-str, red
Jul 2 '09	20	BU191	J W Ray, Liverpool	Ol P	green
Oct 20 '09	12	*DH48	S Vale, Walsall	DAH	tonneau, yellow
Oct 28 '09	12-14	BU205	Rev S L Williamson, Shaw	Ol	side ent, green
Nov 10 '09	25	BU206	Oldham Corporation	Ol	landaulette, then rebodied as an ambulance, dk green
Dec 7 '09	20	BU208	Oldham Corporation	Ol	tourer, light green
Mar 21 '10	20	BU223	Jas Halliwell, Rochdale Rd	Ol	maroon
Mar 24 '10	14	BU226	Brushes Ltd, Southgate St	Ol	delivery cart, red
Apr 11 '10	25	BU231	Oldham Corporation	Ol	landaulette, light green

Date	Horsepower	Regn	First owner and location	Source	Comments
Apr 29 '10	20	AO925	W Holloway, Whitehaven	RGC *P*	side ent tourer, green. 1914 – to J W Ray of L/pool, lorry
May 25 '10	20-24	BU240	Jas Dronsfield, Manor Ho	Ol	limousine, blue/yellow
Jul 13 '10	20	CP178	W Greenwood, Halifax	DAH	van, cream
Jul 15 '10	20	BU252	Dronsfields, Atlas Wks	OL *P*	deliv cart, 19cwt, crimson
Aug 1 '10	8	*BU256	R Eatough, Mossley	Ol	side ent, green (Earlier car)
Aug 17 '10	20	BU257	Eclipse Machine Co	Ol	side ent, green
Sept 8 '10	20	BU260	D Armstrong, Frederick St	Ol	2-str, dark green
Oct 4 '10	20	BU262	Dronsfields, Atlas Wks	Ol *P*	cart, grey, lettered gold
Oct 12 '10	6	*AL1554	G Shepherd, Hucknall, Notts	DAH	2-str, red. (Earlier car)
Dec 19 '10	20	BU269	Buckley & Prockter, Mumps	Ol	van, maroon, lettered gold
Apr 12 '11	25	MN207	M Forrester, Douglas	IoM	landaulette, dk blue (taxi)
Apr 18 '11	20	MN208	W G Hargrave-Thomason, Dgls	IoM	'canary colour' 19cwt
Apr 19 '11	20	BU291	Eclipse Mc Co, A F Rothwell	Ol	4-str, green; later grey
May 9 '11	20	CP215	Wm Greenwood, Halifax		pleasure car, red-brown. The surviving car
May 30 '11	6	*BU299	Sam Cracknell, Glodwick Rd	Ol	2-str, green
Jun 8 '11	15	DK251	Brierley & Kershaw, Roach Wks	Ro	tourer, green
Nov 5 '11	20	*BU77	Levi Francis, Barnsley	Ol	19cwt cab, dark green
Jan 15 '12	20	BU320	S Dodd & Son, Lyon Wks	Ol	landaulette, dark green
Feb 27 '12	20	BU327	Dronsfields, Atlas Wks	Ol	deliv cart, green lettd gold
Mar 21 '12	20	BU333	W F Schofield, Henshaw St	Ol	tourer, yellow/blue
May 1 '12	20	BU344	Thos Fawsitt MRCS, Union St.	Ol	tourer, green, h&s
Jun 21 '12	20	BU355	Eclipse (>J Kemp in May '11)	Ol	torpedo, cream, h&s
Jun 24 '12	20	BU356	Rev S J Williamson	Ol	torpedo, cream, h&s
Aug 23 '12	20	BU372	W A Wright, Brooklands, Sale	Ol	torpedo, green
Aug 27 '12	20	BU373	J T Buckley, Coalshaw Gn Rd	Ol	tourer, grey, h&s
Nov 22 '12	20	EN362	Bury Hospital	DAH	ambulance, varnshd wood
Jan 12 '13	20	BU403	Guardians of the Poor, Oldh'm	Ol	ambulance, varnished
Jul 31 '13	20	BU446	Oldham Indl Co-op, King St	Ol	lorry, det van top, red
Aug 14 '13	20	BU451	Dronsfields, Atlas Wks	Ol	lorry, blue, lettered
Nov 20 '13	20	BU470	Central Meat Co, Manchester	Ol	lorry, red
Jan 5 '14	20	BU481	Wm B Dronsfield, Manor Ho	Ol	2-str, grey
Jan 13 '14	20	BU483	J Collinson & Sons, Halifax	Ol	lorry
Jan 14 '15	20	DK589	St John Ambulance Brigade	Ro *P*	heavy ambulance, 38cwt.
Feb 25 '15	15	BU559	Oldham Corprn C&C Dept	Ol	van, black/lake/green
May 19 '15	15	BU642	Tom Rothwell, Stoneswood	Ol	landaulette, blue
Sept 2 '15	20	BU687	Wm Bowhill, Failsworth	Ol	lorry/landaulette dk green
Sept 15 '15	20	BU689	Alf Ferguson & Co, Hollinghead	Ol	box van, maroon
Sept 20 '15	20	EN718	W Eckersall, Bury	DAH	tourer, grey

Date	Horsepower	Regn	First owner and location	Source	Comments
Oct 25 '15	20	EN724	Red Cross, London	DAH	ambulance
Dec 31 '15	15	BU721	Mrs Frances Rothwell	Ol *P*	landaulette, green. Fred's widow: in many photos
Mar 7 '16	20	BU733	Rochdale Co-op, Lord St, R	Ol	lorry, red, lettered
Sept 25 '16	20	BU766	Dronsfields, Atlas Wks	Ol	lorry, primrose yellow
Jul 25 '17	20	BU822	Guardians of the Poor, Oldham	Ol	lorry, grey
Jul 30 '18	20	BU874	L Brierley & Son, Royton	Ol	lorry, grey
Nov 5 '18	20-25	BU880	Strand Paper Co, Bell Mill	Ol	lorry, green
Jan 7 '19	20	BU894	John B Rothwell, Grendon Av	Ol *P*	4-str, green
Mar 6 '19	15	BU928	Frank & Arthur F Rothwell	Ol	flush side tourer, green
Mar 18 '19	20	BU938	Thos Stone, Erith, Kent	Ol	4-str, grey
Jun 6 '19	20	BU1002	J N Bentley, Windsor Rd	Ol	tourer, green
Jul 7 '19	20	EN983	Fray & Eccles, Radcliffe	DAH	lorry, blue

Printed 21 February 1911

Model	Make of Engine	Cylinders	Bore × Stroke	Capacity	Valves	Ignition	Gearchange	Frame	Wheelbase	Tyres	Current	Notes
6hp		1				Trembler coil	Steering column	Tubular steel		26in	1901 → ?	1
6hp	De Dion	1	90 × 110mm	700cc	AIV	Trembler coil	Side lever quadrant	Tubular steel	6ft 3in		1903 → 6	
8–9hp	De Dion	1	100 × 120mm	943cc	AIV	Trembler coil					1905 → 7	
12hp	Aster Type 26K	2, monobloc	88 × 140mm	1703cc	Side, 'L' head	Trembler coil	Steering column	Ash reinf.	7ft 9in		1903 → 5	2, 7
10–12hp	Aster Type 25LS	2, separate	95 × 130mm	1843cc	Side, 'T' head		Steering column		7ft 9in		1905 → 8	7
10–12hp	Vautour	2, monobloc	100 × 120mm	1885cc	Side, 'L' head	Trembler coil	Steering column	Ash reinf.	6ft 6in		1905 → 8	
12–14hp	White & Poppe	4, separate	80 × 90mm	1810cc	Side, 'T' head	Trembler coil	Side lever	Ash reinf.	8ft 2in or 8ft 6in		1905 → 9	3
15hp	Aster Type 43JS	4, separate	84 × 110mm	2439cc	Side		Side lever quadrant	Pressed steel	9ft 3in	815 × 90	1907 → 8	4
20hp	own	4, pairs	102 × 127mm	4152cc	ohi,se	Dual	Side lever gate	Pressed steel	9ft 3in	815 × 105	1906 → 19	5, 6, 7, 8
15hp	own	4, pairs	79 × 127mm	2353cc	Side	HT magneto	Side lever gate	Pressed steel	9ft 0in	815 × 105	1911 → 19	

Appendix 2
Rothwell Car Models

General comments referring to table on facing page

- Specifications are sparse and sometimes conflicting. The Eclipse Machine Co. was inconsistent in the manner in which they referred to some models.

- Some single and twin cylinder models recorded may have been prototypes, or even have existed only on paper, but have been included.

- All cars had gearboxes with three forward speeds, and all appear to have had leather lined cone clutches. Final drive was by open propeller shaft and bevel rear axle, with two exceptions: the first 6hp cars had single chain drive, and from 1910-12 final drive by side chains was an option on 20hp commercial vehicle chassis.

- Abbreviations: **AIV** = automatic / atmospheric inlet valve; **Ash reinf.** = frame made of ash timber, reinforced with steel flitch-plates; **Dual** = fitted with both trembler coil and high tension magneto ignition systems; **ohi,se** = overhead inlet and side exhaust valves.

Notes

1. It is probable that the engine was a proprietary De Dion-Bouton unit, but that firm's 6hp, 90 x 100mm single cylinder engine was not available as early as November 1901. The most likely engine to have been used was the 4½hp, 84 x 90mm (500cc) De Dion, the Rothwells exaggerating its power output.

2. Also available as a light commercial vehicle. Sometimes referred to as the '12-14hp.'

3. This model seems to have become called the '15hp' by October 1907. A pressed steel frame was introduced from November 1906.

4. The Aster-engined 15hp could be supplied with the trembler coil ignition supplemented by a magneto. Some references quote the cylinder bore at 88mm.

5. At various times and in various sources, the 20hp was referred to as the '20-24hp', '20-25hp', '24hp' '25hp', or '28hp', but all are the same model and share the same engine. In 1907-9, the firm used '20hp' to describe this engine when fitted in the cheaper, lesser specification running gear, and '25hp' when installed in the better and more expensive chassis. In 1910-11, the '25hp' became the '20hp Model A', and the basic 20hp the '20hp Model B'.

6. A tubular front axle was specified for 1909 only – earlier, and subsequently, 'I' section beam front axles were fitted. From 1910, ignition was by HT magneto alone.

7. Solid rubber tyres were an option on commercial Rothwell chassis.

8. By 1910, the basic 20hp model wheelbase was 9ft 6in. The '25hp' (1907-9) then '20hp Model A' (1910 onwards) had a wheelbase 3in longer at 9ft 9in, and 880 x 120 tyres were specified.

Appendix 3

From the *Oldham Chronicle*, 17 August 1904, reproduced with kind permission

Four Oldhamers on a Motor Car
A Pleasant Wakes Week Holiday

A party of four Oldham gentlemen including the owner of a Rothwell motor car of 12hp, made in Oldham, decided upon making a tour in the South of England with the car during the Wakes holidays, and through the kindness of the tourist committee of the Automobile Club of London, an excellent programme was mapped out for them, including some of the prettiest scenery in England.

After seeing the car was supplied with all things likely to be required together with plenty of rugs, waterproofs etc, our tourists left Oldham at 6.10am on Wakes Saturday morning, 27th August 1904 via Manchester, Holmes Chapel, Sandbach, Crewe, Nantwich and Whitchurch, which was reached by 9.30am.

After breakfasting the journey was resumed by them into Shrewsbury. A short stay was made to view Shrewsbury which was left by the magnificent monument erected to Lord Hill. Up to this point the roads had been good and level but now a hillier country was reached, one or two trying hill climbing qualities of the car rather severely. On through an old village called Much Wenlock to Bridgnorth, a fine town which has the appearance of being built upon rocks, after which we skirted a high hill to Kidderminster of carpet fame (3.40pm) and the female workers here it was noted bore a striking resemblance in their dress etc, to Oldham cardroom hands. From here the car bounded away at a great pace on a good road to Worcester which was reached at 4pm and concluded the first day's run of 136 miles.

The party visited the cathedral of that city and enjoyed a walk upon the banks of the beautiful Severn and a tram ride through the city. Sunday morning they were off by 9.45am through Tewkesbury and saw the ruins of its Abbey and its more modern church. The roads were now perfection passing through the land of the orchards of Gloucester. Here a halt was made to view the town and pay a visit to its magnificent cathedral, which inside was temporarily upset by the joiners preparing for the annual music festival. Then on to Stroud, famous for its West of England cloth manufactories, past Dunkirk where the whole neighbourhood teems with evidence of a great Roman encampment in the times of Hadrian II, a beautiful tiled floor being still in existence on the site of an ancient Roman residence. Afterwards we reached the famous town of Bath at 3.40pm. After passing through the party had a wonderful panoramic view of the town with its long terraces and crescents of stately homes. On rising the opposite hill for Warminster, which is a rather large old-fashioned sleepy town; in fact the tourists were struck with the old world beauty of the villages passed through on this glorious route -genuine rustic scenes, such as are seen in the North only on paintings etc. From Warminster was a fine run to Salisbury which completed the second day's run of 104 miles.

Arrived at Salisbury about 6.30pm putting up at the Red Lion. Spent the evening in viewing the old city and was charmed with its world-famed cathedral and its "close" surroundings. This "close" seems to be the boulevard for the inhabitants -a truly delightful spot, well lit up with electric lights at night, the lawns and walks all used as a promenade for a fashionable crowd, overlooked by the towering cathedral itself. Early on Monday morning the motorists were out viewing Salisbury and the Avon again. Then off in the car to Stonehenge across the famous Salisbury plains and downs. Here the great military manoeuvres were in full swing and whilst the Stonehenge ruins were being inspected, our tourist's Oldham motor car became an object of suspicion to some scouting parties on horseback who were on the look-out for some convoy waggons, but after an inspection of the innocent car the soldiers drew away, evidently satisfied it had no connection with the enemy.

Back to Salisbury at 11.00am then off by Ringwood, Wimbourne, past the seat of our late townsman and member, Sir Elliot Lees MP through Dorchester where a stoppage of an hour was made through pump troubles, and it was rather amusing to see some of the party in their shirt sleeves masquerading as amateur mechanics in the main street of Dorchester. The route was one of the finest drives imaginable, long, undulating roads with a splendid surface for motoring. Arrived at Weymouth at 6.30pm (Crown Hotel) having travelled 80 miles only. Afterwards turned out to view Weymouth and were surprised at the beauty of the place, in appearance very much like Douglas, Isle of Man. There was a great change in the weather in the morning.

Hitherto it had been fine and warm, but Tuesday morning was wet and dull. Had a view of Portland and its great prison and saw at anchor around its promontory His Majesty's Home Fleet of men of war. Left Weymouth at l0am for Bournemouth via Preston and Wareham where a stop- page was made for luncheon and repairs to the pump again, about two hours. This time a thorough job was made of the pump and it never gave any further trouble. Good speed was made from here to Bournemouth by excellent roads, arriving at 3.00pm. A stoppage of 1½ hours was made to view some of the beauties of Bournemouth. The motorists were much struck by the natural beauties of the place, its high cliffs, its stately mansions and its beautiful "chines" and gardens etc. On resuming the journey for Southampton the finest drive yet experienced on the tour was enjoyed, in fact by many it was considered the finest road in the Kingdom. It is a road cut right through the New Forest, a long lovely undulating smooth surfaced road, no hedges and but little traffic, and no police. At times at least three miles of road could be seen right away in front and the car sped away at top speed without any hindrance through this lovely country, most exhilarating to all but one, who when asked what was the matter with him said he had been studying where he would stop if a wheel came off. On by Lyndhurst and its common, past the Rt Honourable Sir W V Harcourt's residence to Southampton. Arrived at 6.00pm (Dolphin Hotel), viewed Southampton but found it rather uninteresting from a visitor's point of view. There is a large pier from which steamers are constantly sailing for the Channel ports, Isle of Wight, Cherbourg etc.

Wednesday morning up in good time. Surprised to find the motor car had got a companion stabled with it, viz Sir Thomas Lipton's large 50 horse motor. As it was in good company they left it and took the steamer to the Isle of Wight. A pleasant sail down Southampton harbour where Sir Thomas Lipton's large steam yacht "Erie" was anchored, he having come down from London in his car to join it, also seven large 'Castle' liners were counted in the harbour and five large men of war. Crossed the Solent calling at Cowes, the great yachting centre, the party landing at Ryde and visiting friends there. Ryde is a pretty little town, the whole surroundings being literally a garden. Grapes were found growing outside in the gardens, fruit trees of every kind seeming to groan under their heavy loads of fruit. Returning to Southampton by steamer in a drizzling rain, the journey was resumed by motor car under rather depressing circumstances, the rain coming down in torrents and the roads in places flooded, but the car seemed to make light of all these troubles and dashed and splashed along in fine style, hugging the sea coast and skirting one side of Portsmouth Bay. Although the tourists were well prepared for storms, still the heavy rain, never once abating, began to make travelling uncomfortable, so on arriving at Chichester at five o'clock it was decided to put up at the Dolphin for the night, where there was a good garage for the car which was hardly recognisable under its heavy cloak of mud.

At Chichester there is a very fine cathedral also the remains of a more ancient one and in the centre of the town is a beautifully carved, canopied ancient cross. Late at night Mr C. B. Fry, the famous cricketer and athlete, with his sister, called at the hotel for repairs to his car. He had driven from Hastings and was journeying on to Bournemouth to play in a Gentlemen v Players match next day and, although it was five minutes past midnight when, repairs completed, he left Chichester, his sister driving the car, still he scored 61 runs in the match for the Gentlemen on the following morning. On Thursday morning the party were off for Windsor via Godalming, Guildford, Ripley etc. At times the roads were very hilly, sorely trying the car, but the route was full of interest, richly wooded landscape, dotted here and there with quaint-looking old English homesteads with their heavy dark-coloured tiles or thatching. Stopped for luncheon at the famed Anchor Hotel at Ripley, the popular terminus of the well- known Ripley road run of London cyclists and motorists.

Arrived at Windsor at 4pm. Put up for the night at the White Hart Hotel right opposite the Royal castle and at once, after housing the car, went to visit the home of Royalty. After viewing the lovely scenes from off the ramparts overlooking Eton and the winding Thames, went inside the Castle and saw some of its great treasures. Also got permission to view the west front where the beautiful Italian garden with its fine terrace is situated. This end of the Castle is strictly private except to Oldham motorists, being the residential portion of Royalty, the lookout from the terraces being very fine indeed. Saw the famous three miles drive also the late Queen's mausoleum. After tea took the train for London where the evening was spent.

Friday morning took off by the car again for Stratford-on-Avon, 80 miles via Slough, Eton College, Beaconsfield, whence the late Earl took his title, passed his home Hughenden Manor, by High Wycombe and on by Woodstock, when the car was left outside the park gates whilst the tourists paid a visit to Blenheim Palace. This truly striking piece of architecture was greatly admired, and also its beautiful park, the visitors having a good stroll through it passing the monument on the high pillar of the "Great Duke". Resuming, the route passed through a richly wooded country until Stratford was reached about 6.30pm. After tea, a stroll through the old Shakespearean town; visiting his birthplace etc was very interesting.

Saturday morning started for Ellesmere, 117 miles via Warwick with its great castle, fashionable Leamington, Kenilworth, paying a visit to its fine old castle, having to drive the car through a river to attain this and on by magnificent roads through Coventry, Tamworth and Lichfield, making a stop here to see the cathedral. This cathedral though not so large as some previously visited, was nevertheless one of the prettiest in design, having three spires and the West front contains at least 100 sculptured figures of saints, earthly kings etc: as counted and vouched for by one of the party. Going through Shrewsbury again, arrived at Ellesmere at 7pm. Spent the evening viewing the mere and wandering through the crooked little pleasant town.

Off on Sunday morning at 10.15am for home, 70 miles via Chester and Northwich. Arrived safely at Oldham at 2.25pm having travelled 750 miles through some of the loveliest scenery in England, had little or no trouble with the car except the pump previously mentioned, no accident, never even run over a chicken, but very near running down a pig.

All returned better in health and with a better knowledge of the geography and beauties of their own country after a pleasant and exhilarating run.

A few of the smaller artefacts relating to the Rothwell brothers and the Eclipse Machine Company that are preserved by Julie Dawson.

An advertisement that appeared in January 1911

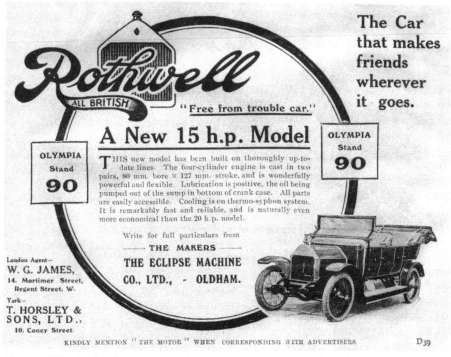

The new 15hp Rothwell is announced, an advertisement of October 1911

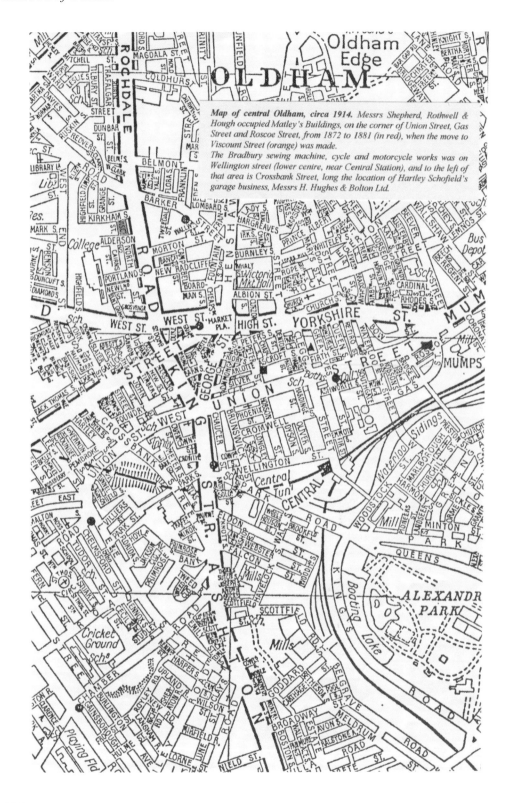

Map of central Oldham, circa 1914. Messrs Shepherd, Rothwell &
Hough occupied Matley's Buildings, on the corner of Union Street, Gas
Street and Roscoe Street, from 1872 to 1881 (in red), when the move to
Viscount Street (orange) was made.
The Bradbury sewing machine, cycle and motorcycle works was on
Wellington street (lower centre, near Central Station), and to the left of
that area is Crossbank Street, long the location of Hartley Schofield's
garage business, Messrs H. Hughes & Bolton Ltd.

Index